The Gardens of
THE NATIONAL TRUST
FOR SCOTLAND

The Gardens of
THE NATIONAL TRUST
FOR SCOTLAND

Francesca Greenoak

Principal photographer:

Brian Chapple

AURUM PRESS

First published 2005
by Aurum Press Ltd,
25 Bedford Avenue, London
WC1B 3AT

Text copyright © 2005
by Francesca Greenoak

Map of the gardens of The
National Trust for Scotland by
ML Design

A catalogue record for
this book is available from the
British Library

ISBN 1 84513 037 5

6 5 4 3 2 1
2010   2009   2008
2007   2006   2005

Printed in Singapore

Opening times, location and
other details of the gardens are
to be found in the National
Trust for Scotland's *Guide to
Properties* guidebook, and at
www.nts.org.uk

Half title page: The thistle at
Leith Hall

Title page: View from the rock
garden at Leith Hall

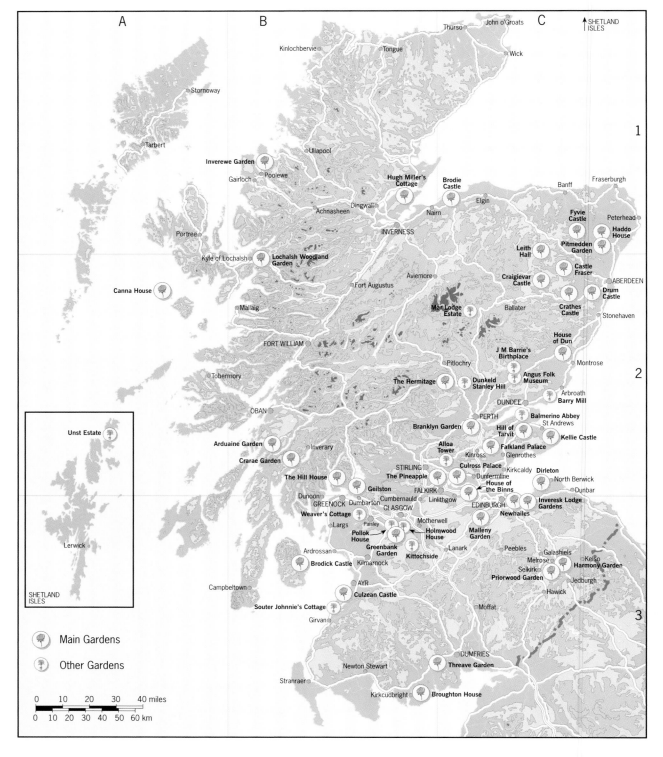

List of Contents

▲ Border at Crathes
Castle
◣ The kitchen garden
at Malleny with its
ornamental basketwork
globes
▶ Branklyn

Introduction

Gardens are a very much more important part of Scottish culture than has generally been allowed. It has only lately been accepted that, from a very early period, substantial and elaborate gardens were a significant means by which affluent Scots expressed their status and esteem.

By 1600 there were more than 100 houses and gardens within a two-mile radius of Edinburgh (noted by the French noble Henri Duc de Rohan, a soldier and writer, and godfather to Charles I of Scotland). There was a gardener employed at the Palace of Holyroodhouse in the early 1500s and maps and other depictions later in the century confirm the presence of well-established royal and private gardens in this area of Edinburgh. Indeed, the parterres reconstructed by The National Trust for Scotland in the garden at Pitmedden, took their inspiration from the depiction of the gardens of Holyrood House in Gordon of Rothiemay's 'Bird's Eye View of Edinburgh' engraved in 1647.

Other 17th-century visitors remarked appreciatively on the range and beauty of Scottish gardens around Edinburgh, Linlithgow, and Glasgow (especially their beautiful orchards) and further afield. Culzean Castle was complimented in 1693 for its 'pretty gardens and orchards', its terraces and walls 'laden with peaches'. The passion for garden-making, at first the preserve of royalty and the aristocracy, was fully shared by the more affluent merchants and men of letters. David Dalrymple, himself soon to buy and transform the landscape of Newhailes, wrote in 1708 to the Earl of Mar, an accomplished architect and landscape designer and genius of the much admired formal garden of Alloa, that visitors 'spok of with delight of everything but the filthy naked statues'. The Earl, said to have been 'infected with the desease of building and gardening' from his youth, also designed two Yorkshire gardens, and had a role in the design of the house and landscape at The House of Dun, overlooking the Montrose Basin, in Angus. He continued to revise and extend plans for the great garden at Alloa even during his years of exile.

Alexander Smith, the 19th-century Scottish

The ornamental kitchen garden at Malleny with the charming woven basket globes

poet-essayist, writing of a fictional Linlithgow, observed 'How deeply seated in the human heart is the liking for gardens and gardening.' Time and again in his writing he remarks how strongly this sentiment was shared by villagers and the urban poor, as well as by the wealthy. He also loved the way gardens 'fitted within their landscape', a quality particularly important for gardens in Scotland for practical quite as much as aesthetic and symbolic reasons.

SCOTTISH GARDENS

Most people can name a few Scottish gardens: perhaps Inverewe, Crathes, Crarae or Culzean; but fewer recognise that these celebrated landmarks are part of a pattern of history and horticulture that

dates back many centuries. This book is about the gardens and designed landscapes cared for by The National Trust for Scotland, which with their wide regional spread represent a selection of different form, period and complexity.

The remarkable plants of the west-coast gardens, where climate is softened by the warm waters of the North Atlantic Drift are justly celebrated as are other more southerly gardens such as Threave, and Broughton House, in Kirkcudbright. Gardens of the 18th-century gentry of Edinburgh and the Lothians such as Inveresk and Malleny are now treasures within a built-up environment. There is remarkable richness and beauty in northeasterly gardens such as Crathes Castle and Pitmedden. Up in Cromarty, I sat basking in sunshine one day in the delightful small garden of Hugh Miller's Cottage. There is Canna House, on the most westerly of the Small Isles in the Inner Hebrides. The most northerly of the Trust's gardens are Halligarth and Old House of Lund on Unst in the north of Shetland.

GARDEN HISTORY

Scottish gardens differ from those of the rest of the British Isles historically as well as geographically. Scotland retained stronger links with mainland Europe in the 17th and 18th centuries. The great libraries, the most significant of which was that at Newhailes, contained French and Dutch gardening books and there was a continuous two-way flow of cultural influence. Most Scottish castles more closely resemble French chateaux than their English counterparts. The French and Dutch influence, possibly coupled with unstable politics, and an inclination to maintain houses that looked like

Border at Crathes Castle

fortresses, entailed a different kind of development. Exuberant features such as crow-stepped or corbie gables, bartizans, elaborate sundials and doocots were features of Scottish estates, which took on a new life in the flourishing of the Scottish Baronial style in the 19th century.

Investigating a garden involves uncovering political, social and cultural history, as well as horticultural high points. The National Trust for Scotland has commissioned landscape surveys that do exactly this for several of its gardens, and it is hoped that it can gradually do the same for all of them. These surveys are not regarded as the last word, but more as a body of information that can be continuously refined and augmented. It will be exciting to see what more garden archaeology might reveal about the medieval history, absorbed by, or covered over by, later developments.

PLANTS

The plants of Scottish gardens have always delighted and surprised visitors — even John Ray the eminent botanist, visiting in 1662, was gratified to encounter species he had not seen before. He praised Edinburgh gardens and expressed surprise to see in Linlithgow 'divers exotick plants, more than one would hope to find in so northerly and cold a country'. Contemporary observations and estate accounts, where available, and plant lists of the period were used as a basis for the reconstruction and planting of period gardens, such as the 17th-century garden at Culross Palace. Lists of plants from mid-18th-century Scottish gardens show as full a complement of plants as comparably fashionable English gardens, and as new plants

XIII

One of two sphinxes
that used to look over
the Sheep Park at
Newhailes

began to arrive from America and the Himalaya
(many brought in by Scots) they found welcoming
terrain and skills to grow them in Scottish gardens.

There is a particular quality to the planting of
Scottish gardens. The plants in garden borders:
filipendulas, rogersias, eremurus lilies for example,
come rapidly to a strikingly tall, robust and shapely
maturity in the relatively short growing season and
long summer days.

Outsiders tend to think of cold as the main
impediment to gardening in Scotland, but, in general,
gardeners today will tell you that they suffer more
from winds and waterlogging than cold. Most soils
in Scotland are acid, which means fewer problems
with mollusc damage and a good ground for
heathers, rhododendrons and a host of exotic
acid-loving plants. Flowering shrubs such as a wide
range of species of orange blossom *Philadelphus*,
are especially well grown and beautiful in form —
and new Chinese species continue to be discovered
and planted.

Some plants that grow particularly well in
Scotland, such as Himalayan poppies and primroses,
have a special association with certain gardens:
there is *Meconopsis* 'Branklyn' and the striking red
Primula 'Inverewe'.

Most gardens in Scotland are placed so as to catch
the sun and to give shelter from wind, so you find
many on south-facing slopes on hillsides or sloping
valley bottoms. Over centuries, Scots gardeners
have built up skills in the positioning of walls and
hedges, and especially in planting shelter belts. The
art is still developing: some of the trees put in
during the 19th century are now considered to cast
too much shade, or to self-seed too vigorously.

Trees are grown both for timber and for their
beauty. Many planted in the late 18th and 19th
centuries have now reached a splendid maturity.

Almost all the larger gardens have associated woodland, and it is a joy to walk through the woods along
the River Braan at The Hermitage, and through the
mixed woodland at Crathes where some of the
beeches and oaks are breathtaking. Along the west
coast, gardens are known for their rhododendron
collections, and for unusual and showy trees and
shrubs such as enkianthus and olearias. Other
exotic trees such as eucryphias and leptospermums
make exceptional growth.

Over the past decade or so the gardens at Trust
properties have become as much a focus of public
interest as the castles and houses. Some properties,
notably Pitmedden, Inverewe, Crarae and Lochalsh
and Arduaine — where no associated house is open
to the public — nonetheless attract a large and loyal
following of visitors. There are other properties
where house and garden are so completely integrated,
it is difficult to think of one without the other.
Kellie Castle, for many decades the home of the
Lorimer family, is a fine example.

The Trust has been responsible for recreating
or originating some gardens, such as the reconstruction of a period garden behind the small,
beautifully intact 17th-century Culross Palace and
at Hugh Miller's Cottage, where a garden of great
charm tumbles around the home of the celebrated
geologist and evangelical journalist who loved wild
flowers. Almost all the other gardens have new or
restored developments integrated with or alongside
the historic designs, the beautiful woodland cliff
garden at Crathes Castle, or the orderly garden of
Scottish fruits being implemented at Fyvie Castle,
for example.

While gardens brought into the Trust's care,
necessarily have national significance, they each
have an individual character that is highly valued.
They are managed by a group of head gardeners of

considerable skill and intelligence who have the responsibility for guiding the gardens into the future, in consultation with the three Regional Advisers and the Head of Gardens. The remit is to look after the gardens with respect to their history and context, which given the way that gardens themselves grow and change means in practice to develop the 21st-century phase of that garden.

GARDENS AND GARDENERS

Gardens are always part of the fabric of the society and the horticultural period from which they emerged, and they are also the expressions of the personal tastes of individuals, families, or a series of owners. Several generations of Dalrymples created Newhailes; the Lorimers rehabilitated Kellie Castle; the painter Edward Atkinson Hornel made a highly wrought, Japanese-inspired town garden at Broughton House in Kirkcudbright, and starting from scratch at Branklyn, husband and wife Dorothy and John Renton perfected the skills of growing unusual plants within a beautifully organised design.

This is the first book to explore the gardens of The National Trust for Scotland as a group. It is my personal impression of the gardens as they are at the beginning of the 21st century and it deals with them in the context of present day developments in garden history, horticulture and society. Increased awareness of the importance of gardens for the natural world is now an important element in Trust conservation. Conserving old and unusual cultivars is also of concern and The National Trust for Scotland holds a number of National Plant Collections under the auspices of the NCCPG (National Council for the Conservation of Plants

Rosa 'Westerland' and *Eccremocarpus scaber* 'Carmineus' at Drum Castle

and Gardens) and it is likely that the number will increase. Research on the qualities of original plant accessions (past and recent) is also being pursued.

These gardens are more than the sum of their principal features, or their botanical or cultural significance, each is a distinctive, living, work of art, whose purpose is to delight the senses. This book may tempt you to visit the gardens described – your experience will be a personal one and it will be unique.

Branklyn Garden

Branklyn, on the west-facing slopes of the bank of the River Tay in Perthshire, was a small orchard when Dorothy and John Renton bought land for a house and small garden there in 1922. At first their territory stretched only a little beyond the house, but over 40 years, as their interest in collecting and designing with special plants grew, they increased the size of the garden until it reached its present size of the 0.7 hectare.

The couple gardened in partnership: Dorothy had a keen interest in botany, John considered himself the designer. Dorothy knew the importance of finding out about a plant's natural habitat, and employed this understanding to grow rarities that professional gardeners had difficulties with. Form followed function in the garden, and the terraces, screes, and woodland glades, were all carefully designed and assembled for the plants they were to accept. With so many plants from all over the world available to us now, it takes an effort of imagination to understand the extraordinary excitement in horticulture in the first half of the 20th century. China was open to exploration by

7

plant-hunters and huge quantities of new plants were being sent back to Europe.

Many of these came from mountainous regions and the passion for rock gardens developed as a response. Reginald Farrer whose expeditions furnished many of the plants that came to Branklyn was concerned both for aesthetics and for the health of the plants, giving clear instructions about how to construct artificial mountain conditions, and deploring most attempts as horrible. The Rentons also had plant materials from George Forrest's expeditions, and were actually subscribers to his last one, in 1931. Interestingly, the vast majority of the Renton's collection was grown from seed. Dorothy was careful in her treatment of the seeds, using knowledge and ingenuity to persuade them to germinate, giving the seedlings optimum conditions, then choosing the best for the garden. Her displays of *Paraquilegia anemonoides* with its small blue anemone-shaped flowers, and feathery blue-green foliage 'the finest cliff plant of the whole range' according to Forrest himself, were astonishing in her day, and still draw comment.

Branklyn's plants came principally from the Himalayas: Tibet, Bhutan, and China. Dorothy understood that, for many of them, a good free-draining rock scree would mean the difference between surviving or not. She used different means to make the soil at Branklyn, which was a medium to light loam over a rocky substrate, more montane-like. For the first rock garden in 1925, the Rentons brought rocks from a disused Kinoull quarry further up the hill. At first it looked like a Mars land-

scape, but a gravel and loam mixture was added and topped with a layer of pure gravel which suited the plants well and soon began to look quite natural.

It is difficult to appreciate the passion of this period for rock gardens from the perspective of the present time, when we are almost religiously opposed to them. There are good conservation reasons for not removing huge quantities of stone from their native parts, not least the degradation of the original habitat. The Rentons, living in a naturally rocky area, had perhaps more justification than many, and at least they used local rock and river gravel. In effect, the garden at Branklyn is a piece of history, a historical artefact of living material that will never be reproduced. Dorothy Renton's notebooks give us an insight into how new plant material was received and cared for, and many of the plants are themselves the originals or direct decendents of those that first came into Western Europe.

▲ Early days: Mrs Dorothy Renton, gardener and spaniel

▶ A bold Renton combination of orange tiger lily *Lilium lancifolium* and *Hydrangea paniculata*
◀ Maple *Acer palmatum* Dissectum Atropurpureum Group

▲ The maple path. The purple of the maple *Acer palmatum* var. *rubrum* contrasts well with the foliage of the golden cedar, *Cedrus atlantica* v. 'Aurea'. The golden cedar had its leader shoot removed at an early stage so that a spreading tree was formed

▶ The scree rock garden, originally a tennis court, with alpines and dwarf shrubs that all require excellent drainage and a sunny site

Some of the new plants originated in limestone regions of China or European limestone regions, so one rock garden area had limestone added. Dorothy Renton grew her famously thriving paraquilegia here. Pasque flowers also like this habitat, as do some gentians and saxifrages.

Branklyn has always been renowned for the density and skill of its planting. Species from different parts of the world do not always look well together, in fact rather the opposite, but Dorothy was skilled in placing plants for tone and texture. Graham Stuart Thomas thought it perfection: 'everything was placed to provide the utmost beauty from it, associated with its neighbours.' By all accounts the Rentons enjoyed their visitors and were most welcoming and generous. No plant-loving visitor would leave without a few plant treasures, and instructions about how to care for them.

It is estimated that there are upwards of 3500 different kinds of plant at Branklyn, and careful gardening on the part of The National Trust for Scotland has ensured that the richness continues. The garden came to the Trust on the death of John Renton in 1967, a year after his wife died, and it has been a point of principle to garden it as closely as possible in the Renton style. The originators of the garden were themselves keen to have flowers all through the season and encouraged visitors, so the idea of sharing its beauty was already in the spirit of the garden, though the scale was to be vastly increased as more and more visitors beyond the specialist gardening coterie came to know about it through the Trust.

The garden opens on All Fools' Day when several kinds of hellebore have already been blooming for some while and the trilliums are just beginning their superb sequence with the stern, deep-red beauty of *Trillium sessile* at its best, contrasting with the large white-flowered *Trillium grandiflorum* in both single and double forms and the pink-hearted *Trillium rivale*. Flowering primulas are also much in evidence including unusually free-seeding oxlips, which grow in the beds and seem to delight in the gravel paths. The Bhutan primrose: small, many-flowered and pale mauve, is one of the first to bloom on the scree. The larger cultivar 'Old Port' glows deep crimson-brown alongside the dwarf rhododendron *Rhododendron forrestii* which has glorious deep crimson flowers. Branklyn has many erythroniums. The pretty pink North American species *Erythronium revolutum* has naturalised spectacularly in shady places all over the garden, and there are contrasting clumps of *Erythronium*, 'Pagoda' and *E. revolutum* 'White Beauty'. The North Series of Asiatic hybrid lilies are a new departure. A collection of these beautiful lilies, which were raised in nearby Dundee, is gradually being integrated into the garden.

Branklyn has from its inception been a changing, developing garden. Graham Stuart Thomas described how 'shrubs and trees as they grew to maturity altered the banks and levels from warm sunny places to cool shady positions'. The Rentons, he noted, 'had to be continually on the lookout to see whether new sites required planting or under-planting needed to be moved to a more desirable position.' This continual reassessment goes on in any garden, but more so when there are rare plants and collections whose requirements are critical. Branklyn is not large, so the mature size of larger plants is also a significant factor. Conifers planted as 'dwarf' can get very large after several decades, changing the habitat around them and altering proportion within the garden. Several of these have been removed over the decades. Even rare rhodo-dendrons don't stand still and in the early months of

▲ *Rhododendron kiusianum* with dwarf cornel *Cornus canadensis* growing beneath

◀ Orchids *Dactylorhiza foliosa* from Madeira

▲ *Meconopsis napaulensis* hybrids with the Japanese snowball bush *Viburnum plicatum* 'Mariesii'

◥ *Rhododendron griffithianum* hybrid on the lower path by the Tibetan cherry

▶ *Lilium nepalense* grows well in the cool climate of Perthshire

2004 a large bush of the cultivar 'Temple Belle' that had gradually taken up a whole bed, was removed. This opened up quite a large area in the southern part of the garden for replanting. 'Temple Belle', which is a beautiful rhododendron with round evergreen leaves and elegant trusses of clear pink flowers, had earlier been propagated and a smaller plant was ready as a replacement.

There is a concern for texture and shape as well as colour in the garden and it is suprising how many large shrubs and trees make a contribution.

Selective planting means that they also give the impression that the garden is larger and more secluded than it actually is, only a little way above what has now become a fairly busy road. There are several plants of *Viburnum plicatum* 'Mariesii' although its characteristic tiered effect has been a little modified by pruning. The shining coppery bark of the trunk of *Prunus serrula* grows at a place close to a path where the sun catches it and it looks its best. Perhaps the best known large tree in the garden, the birch *Betula albosinensis* var. *septentrion-*

alis collected by Joseph Rock in China (1927), is famous for its attractive pink-tinged bark. The original tree is now one of the largest in Britain, but birches are not long-lived and there is another (a self-seeded youngster) earmarked for the day a replacement is required.

The maple-bordered path at the upper western part of the garden is a high point of interest, both for its historic value and its beauty – but even small maples grow and the overhanging branches of the trees were being damaged by people walking the path. The solution in this case has been to close the path to foot traffic, but to have places where the vista can be viewed from either end. The small far-eastern maples, greeted with delight and astonishment when they first came to the west, continue to be appreciated even though these small dainty trees have become staples of our gardens. The famed original accessions at Branklyn which belong to the filigree-leaved Dissectum Group of *Acer palmatum*, always attract autumn visitors eager to see their fabulous purples, golds and crimsons. At the heart of the garden another maple, *Acer shirasawanum* 'Aureum', opens a bright golden green, turning red before leaf fall.

In addition to the historic plants first grown at in this garden, there are many specialities including the dark blue *Meconopsis* (George Sherriff Group) 'Branklyn'. There is also a paeony 'Branklyn', an outstanding plant still to be named officially in the cultivated plant register. Perhaps a few plants that are still not widely grown such as the gorgeous hybrid Asiatic lilies. The lily-like notholirions, should also have a mention, and one of my favourites a claret-coloured *Corydalis solida*. Though a modest plant, the genus *Cassiope* should also be noted, as Branklyn holds the National Collection of these little ericaceous shrubs with

▲ A *Meconopsis* called 'Dorothy Renton' in the George Sherriff group, with a *Rhododendron griffithianum* hybrid.
▶ A branchlet of *Cassiope stelleriana*

their tiny round-belled flowers. There is so much to see at Branklyn at any time of the year, that even the pampered gardeners of today are spoilt for choice. The charm of this garden lies not so much in the enumeration of its plants but the way each individual perceives them. This is a garden of enormous riches, made to be appreciated intimately and personally, so each of us carries away a recollection special to ourselves.

Brodick Castle

The traveller voyaging from Ardrossan sees the Isle of Arran gradually resolve into recognisable features: one of the most distinctive being the red sandstone of Brodick Castle, its woods and castle parks on the hillsides of the east side of the bay, with Goatfell mountain behind it. The designed landscape of Brodick is integral to the first impressions of Arran. The castle is built on an ancient raised beach with its formal gardens sloping gently to the south, the remarkable field systems of the Castle Parks and the great woodlands enclosing it. Irregularities in the ground, created by the retreating glacier, make the woodlands rocky and exciting especially along the walks created around the three burns that run through Brodick.

During the floods of 2004, the burns were swollen into torrents, spectacularly crashing through the woodlands of oak, ash, beech, pines, and exotic rhododendrons and temperate forest trees. If you allow yourself to enjoy the rain and mist, there is

◀◀ View over the walled garden, and the rose circle
◀ The west façade with its 19th-century tower by James Gillespie and *Fuchsia* 'Mrs Popple'

enchantment in such conditions, the beautiful tree trunks gleaming, and water dripping from the great rhododendron leaves. Even in sunny weather, you are never far from the sound of running water, or the sea, and the scents of the plants and the moist earth.

The walled formal gardens, in contrast, have a quiet ordered aspect. They were reconstructed in 1982, using as a guide photographs from the 1920s that show pleasure gardens with a graceful design of borders of late 19th-century style. The present garden is beautifully executed, with a lightness of touch in its introduction of new plants that gives balance to the parts. A circular garden in the lower section provides an opportunity for delightful plant combinations such as green nicotiana and verbena providing scent and delicate contrast in colour. There used to be a rose garden and pavilion in this position. This walled garden, built in 1710, was originally the kitchen garden but when the Hamilton family began to use Brodick Castle as their main residence in the mid-19th century, a new kitchen garden was made in the walled tree-nursery by Cladach beach to the southwest.

A magnificent bay laurel, in the upper part of the castle walled garden is believed to be the only plant to survive from the old garden. Many tender plants, including eucryphias, acacias and large New Zealand leptospermums and pittosporums thrive here. The climate is excellent for many herbaceous plants not considered hardy, such as diascias, penstemons and tall watsonias (adopted by the Botanical Society of the British Isles as the name for its journal).

Through the doorway at the end of the walled garden, you drop to the ponds and lush growth of the lower garden, lit up in spring by the reds, carmines and golds of the candelabra primulas. Hostas, vast-leaved gunneras, hydrangeas, ferns and rare cobra lilies *Darlingtonia californica*, pitcher plants from North America, grow in the boggy conditions. One of the most striking rarities in this area is the graceful Chinese form of the Himalayan juniper *Juniperus recurva* var. *coxii* with its long drooping needles and cinnamon-red bark. Further downhill towards the sea, you begin to meet the large-leaved rhododendrons that are such a charac-teristic of Brodick (*R. sinogrande*, *R. maccabeanum*, *R. protistum* and *R. falconeri*) each with its distinctive leaf and flower form.

The Bavarian Summer House looking out over the woodland and to the sea, was made in 1845 for Princess Marie of Baden, wife of the 11th Duke of Hamilton. It is the sole survivor of four of these rus-tic structures she built at strategic places in the wood-land gardens. The wooden building is decorated inside with patterns of pine, cedar and fir cones, and outside with twisted stems of *Rhododendron ponticum*.

Adventurous walkers can climb narrow, rocky steps following a path designed to recapture the experience of plant-collectors, whose travels con-tributed so much to this garden. You duck under large branches, brush by foliage and climb along rocky ledges, make your way over high walkways and narrow wooden bridges among the tree ferns, *Dicksonia antarctica*, and rare rhododendrons such as *Rhododendron pendulum* growing in and under the overhanging rocks and ledges. The walk is punctuated by panels with quotations from the plant collector Frank Kingdon Ward that bring home both how laborious and how thrilling his expedi-tions must have been.

It was raining harder than ever now, and forcing our way through drenched bushes we were soon wet to the skin; water streamed off us, and my feet were perishingly cold. How I hated the whole business . . .

◀ *Rhododendron* 'Polyroy'

▶ *Wisteria sinensis* blooms over the arbour

◀ The pocket handkerchief tree, *Davidia involucrata*

▶ *Primula* 'Rowallane Rose'

The walled garden
in 1896

But there were seeds I must get or perish in the effort. It was simply unthinkable to return without them.

The sand-loam soil and humidity of this part of the garden make it possible to grow rhododendrons and magnolias that would fail almost anywhere else in Britain. Among the more difficult and unusual species are *Rhododendron protistum* a large tree with big leaves and the small, very tender, scented *R. nuttallii*. Brodick's rhododendrons are planted skilfully so that the trees and shrubs blend together in naturalistic combination.

The Duchess of Montrose began to introduce exotica along the gorges of Brodick's wooded burns in the 1920s. Her Hamilton ancestors had begun substantial planting of woods from the 18th century onwards. Marie of Baden had made the romantic woodland walks, thereby providing a context for the exotics of her grand-daughter. The Duchess planted for beauty of plant association, attempting also to recreate the natural habitat of the plants and during the 1920s and 30s achieved a remarkably

similar effect, which the Trust is intent to preserve.

The spring blossom is stunning, especially since many of Brodick's rhododendrons are scented, but the leaves, white or brown felted on the underside, or glossy and rounded make the walks attractive at any time of year, especially when the trunks are glistening brown, red, or purple. You don't have to know the names to enjoy the architecture and individual detail of these splendid plants.

Rhododendrons and other plants came to Brodick from famous plant expeditions, led by Kingdon Ward, George Forrest, Reginald Farrer and Joseph Rock. The original acquisitions of the early 20th century have been augmented by gifts of plants from Tresco in the 1930s (Thomas Algernon Dorrien-Smith of Tresco was uncle to the Duchess of Montrose's gardening companion, her son-in-law John Boscawen). Sir James Horlick whose island garden on Gigha is renowned for its rhododendrons (the plants now owned by the National Trust for Scotland) sent a gift of rhododendrons in 1962. In recent years, Brodick has been fortunate in having head gardeners who have themselves increased the garden's riches, through expeditions to China, South America and Australasia.

Many tender and difficult plants self-seed generously at Brodick. Hybrids abound alongside original plantings and others raised from seed. Some plants are individually distinctive enough to have earned cultivar names such as subspecies *R. arizelum* 'Brodick' which has purple-pink flowers with a dark crimson blotch. A version of the yellow-flowered rhododendron, *R. luteiflorum* called locally 'Glen Coy' or a large *R. arboreum* which has tawny brown bark, called 'Goat Fell' after the mountain above Brodick.

It is well worth reserving time to walk to the Cnocan Burn 350m to the west of the castle, where a walk leads alongside the rocky burn, as it travels through a richly wooded gorge that narrows to a thunderous waterfall. There are fine trees, rhododendrons and beautiful ferns favoured by the humid conditions alongside the burn. Among the dozen different kinds is the filmy fern *Hymenophyllum tunbrigense*, hardly ever seen outdoors in Britain.

The Mill Burn walk is within easy reach of the castle, leading you around to the Horlick collection. Designed by Princess Marie to cross and recross the burn, it was known as the Seven Bridges Walk, and has been partly restored. This walk gives an idea of how expansive the landscape of Brodick is and how is it is able to encompass very different plant communities. Nearby also is one of the finest trees in the garden a most beautifully shaped mature southern beech, *Nothofagus dombeyi*, a Balfour introduction, from the higher slopes of the Chilean Andes. The path leads to a viewpoint over the sea – one of several that are being restored – and plunges incongruously into an impressive eucalyptus grove.

The Merkland Burn runs to the sea to the east of the castle, through some of the finest woodland on the estate. For those who like a long hike, the Merk Burn walk is connected to that of Cnocan by a long route called the Balmoral Ride, constructed in the 1860s by Princess Marie.

The many well known designers who have surveyed Brodick include John Burrel (1770s and 1780s), W.A. Nesfield (1850s) and Reginald Blomfield (1919). Other notable names such as Thomas White junior, and W.H. Playfair were approached or made visits. None of their proposals was carried out. A version of some of John Burrel's radical reforms was put in place, notably the Castle Parks which made six enclosures, replacing (but not totally obscuring) the old clachan strip-farming and common grazing, in a large area visible above the castle. Carried out for

▸ Self-seeded *Papaver orientale*
◢ Skunk cabbage *Lysichiton americanus* and *Gunnera manicata*

agricultural reasons, it made a big difference to vistas of Brodick. Although Nesfield's revolutionary changes were ignored, apart from the institution of the approach drive from the east in the 1850s, shelterbelt and woodland planting continued in the late 18th and 19th centuries. Blomfield's ideas were entirely rejected. The family was interested in design, but seemed to prefer an incremental approach, and the advice of friends. Napoleon III may have influenced Princess Marie's development of the romantic wooded walks, picturesque incidents and views (they were cousins). He visited her and they corresponded on the subject. She was also considerably helped by the landscape artist George Hering (whose view of Brodick Bay hangs in the castle). The Duchess of Montrose certainly appreciated the advice of her son-in-law and fellow plant enthusiast J.P.T. Boscawen in her planting of exotics.

The castle that looks down over the terraces and old walled garden has undergone changes, ruination and augmentation since it was first built in the 13th century. Some of the ancient fabric survives in the lower parts of walls by the steps, but it is principally a mid 19th-century building by James Gillespie Graham, built for the 10th and 11th Dukes of Hamilton.

Visitors come to Brodick as much for the gardens as for the castle and its Beckford treasures, but it is still to some extent a sleeping beauty. The walks are gradually being opened and vistas renewed, but the significance of its horticultural wealth (already attested to by two collections of rhododendrons) should surely be comprehensively recorded and more widely recognised.

▲ Cobra lilies *Darlingtonia californica* American pitcher plants with other damp-loving plants

Brodie Castle

The path to the castle leads through dark forest to the sudden bright openness of lawn from which the creamy lime-harled castle, with its fairytale turrets and crowstepped gables, rises, beautiful and impressive. It gives an impression of past grandeur and high style. A huge copper beech almost as high as the castle leads the eye to others in a generous tree-lined avenue in the French manner, opening on to the lake at its furthest point.

There have been ornaments and extensions but, Brodie Castle, high in the northeast, not far from Inverness, is firmly in the tradition of Scottish fortified houses of the 16th century, with its tower house and square towers, ornate battlements and bartizans. The date 1567 is carved on the caphouse of the southwest tower and it is thought that the west wing was added during the 17th century; but in 1645 the estate was 'byrnt and plunderit' by the Royalists

◀◀ Winter skies over the daffodil trial grounds in the walled garden
◀ Daffodil 'Cotterton' one of the most vigorous and reliable of the Brodie cultivars

21

A swathe of naturalised daffodils on the main avenue.

though most of the building survived, and underwent few changes for the better part of a century.

Though only one great avenue remains, there is a sense of spaciousness and, perhaps, phantoms of the radiating avenues of the ambitious 18th-century design that was put in place by Alexander Brodie of Brodie the 19th laird and his wife Mary Sleigh. In their plan, (clearly delineated on an estate map dated 1769) the line of the avenue continued formally along a canal to a circular lake. They also cre-

ated a wilderness, and a serpentine drive approaching the castle from the south, also rather French, but these no longer survive. The avenue was in the shape of an arrow (the crest of the Brodie coat of arms is an arm holding three arrows.) The fletch came to a point at the castle, widening to a triangle, the rest of the avenue and canal making the shaft This area has closed in and the lake is now informal but as the trees die back over the course of time, the original shape will be gradually restored.

Two more Brodie narcissi ◀◀ 'Suda' and ◀ 'Seraglio'

The 19th Earl's refashioning of the house and grounds was costly and the estate was impoverished for many decades until William, the 22nd Earl, commissioned a major extension of the castle from William Burn in 1824. About a third of the enlargement was carried out, and then altered by William Wylson who added the entrance hall and library and remade the gables in the Scottish crowstep style. Known as Brodie House for most of its life, it was retitled under the influence of the Scottish romanticism of the Victorian period.

The mid-19th century saw a reworking of the grounds, a softening of the formal canal and basin, and extensive planting of wellingtonias, monkey puzzle trees and other fashionable conifers new to horticulture. The Shrubbery to the east of the castle is a surviving part of this era of planting. Some fine trees, notably boundary specimens such as Sitka spruce, redwood, sycamore and a Nootka cypress *Chamaecyparis nootkatensis*, stand out among well-grown shrubs and smaller trees. Many of these originated in Japan or North America: the Pacific dog-

wood *Cornus nuttallii*, *Pieris japonica* and *Stewartia pseudocamellia* and numerous rhododendrons. Some of these rhododendrons were seedlings raised from the original expeditions. They were given to Ian, the 24th Brodie of Brodie, and closely observed to see whether they would grow well in a garden so far north (Brodie Castle is 24 miles northeast of Inverness). Notes from the Rhododendron Society in 1925 give details of *Rhododendron falconeri* and *R. yunnanense* and others surviving 20^{0}F and no doubt the Earl would be gratified to know that a good proportion still thrive at Brodie. Wild and naturalised flowers (including species narcissus) planted in the 19th century, grow still in the grass under the trees in this pleasant enclosure.

The large walled garden some distance away from the castle to the east, was also a development of this 19th century period. Some espalier apple and pear trees survive from a productive period that extended into the 1940s, although by then, they shared the nearly 2-hectare enclosure with a developing daffodil collection.

Daffodil 'Dallas'

In the 20th century, achievement was principally horticultural. Ian, the 24th Brodie of Brodie, was a pioneer in daffodil breeding, fortunate to have a wife, Violet, who shared his passion for daffodils. He raised about 25,000 varieties, naming over 440 of them. His work had considerable influence on the style and form of garden daffodils. His bulbs were planted in precise rows in the walled garden, his first efforts directed at the golden yellow 'King Alfred' forms, of which 'Ben Avon' is an excellent example. An important development was the acquisition of 'Fortune' from a fellow breeder. He realised the importance of this cultivar, which had a reliably stable orange coloured cup. From it, come most of the daffodils of this colouration including Ian Brodie's own 'Lethen'. He also raised white trumpeted forms. 'Dallas' is a white, late-flowering narcissus with a remarkable green centre. His pink-trumpeted, white daffodils, of which 'Helena Brodie' is a good example, were a sensation. The personal favourite of David Wheeler, the Head Gardener, is 'Daviot', with white petals, setting off an orange trumpet, streaked with yellow.

Daffodils were recently planted down the great west avenue presenting a dazzling display in spring. If to a botanist or garden historian, this seems an

Ian Brodie, the 24th Brodie of Brodie examining some daffodils in his trial beds in the walled garden

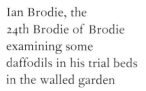

incongruous combination of an 18th-century avenue and large-bloomed, mid-20th-century garden daffodils, the effect is undeniably brilliant, and appreciated by the many visitors to the Brodie parkland. Plants have a way of settling to suit their surroundings, and it will be interesting to see how this avenue will look in future decades.

Ninian, the 25th Brodie of Brodie, spent many happy years at the Castle with his wife Helena and their children. In 1980, he transferred the whole 71-hectare estate into the care of The National Trust for Scotland. The Trust has begun restoring the west avenue and some of the *patte d'oie* paths and tree belts to their original proportions. David Wheeler has made great inroads into identifying the named cultivars of the substantial and significant daffodil collection which he is responsible for maintaining, and which is registered with the NCCPG as the National Plant Collection of Brodie daffodils.

A walk to the lake is an experience that flips you alternately through past and present. As you stroll down the wide 18th-century avenue with its tall Scots pine, limes and beech trees, with buzzards soaring above, your gaze is arrested intermittently by vehicles that appear at a distance to be gliding across the water, but are actually passing along a hidden road between the avenue and the lake. Anyone making a circuit through the attractive mixed woodland paths edging the lake, will find birds and wild plants – and the occasional thundrous roar of a train that shatters the peace for a few seconds as it passes along the line by the western boundary. It might be argued that the historic landscape of Brodie should have been isolated from these intrusions, but the disruption is marginal, and they could also be seen as part of a long and continuing process of adaptation.

'Helena Brodie' the trumpet fringed with pink

◀ The Shrubbery which contains a range of fine trees as well as flowering shrubs. Daffodils were planted here in the 19th century.

Broughton House

Broughton House is a domestic treasure. Numbers 10 and 12 High Street, Kirkcudbright, combined, made an expansive town house, the home and garden of the celebrated painter Edward Atkinson Hornel. He was a member of the group of artists, active about the turn of the 20th century, known as the Glasgow Boys who brought new life to the artistic landscape of Scotland.

E.A. Hornel moved to the substantial 18th-century Broughton House fronting on to an elegant street in his home town of Kirkcudbright in the early 20th century, (he had been brought up just a few houses along at number 18). Broughton House was built for (and took its name from) the Murrays of Broughton and Cally, in 1740. Hornel bought it in 1901, clearly attracted by its nice proportions,

◀◀ *Girls picking blue flax* by Edward Atkinson Hornel (*c.* 1900) Hornel had an interest in wild and garden plants. Brighouse Bay not far from Broughton house is the only place in Scotland where this flax grows wild.

◀ A granite quern filled with gazanias, on a millstone with Japanese anemones *Anemone hupehensis*, Lady's mantle and *Crocosmia* 'Lucifer' behind

◀ Two views into the Japanese garden. The canna shares its pot with pink verbena.

▶ *Yucca gloriosa*

and outbuildings that, by 1909, he had converted into a gallery and studio. At the rear is a garden stretching down to the estuary of the River Dee.

Once the rebuilding was finished he could turn his thoughts to the garden, making a beautifully idiosyncratic masterpiece that employed his artistry in a different sphere. As early as 1907, he was writing that his garden 'has been doing marvels'. In it he explored the possibilities of a Japanese-style garden in a Scottish context. An interest in Japanese art and garden design, engendered within the European artistic community at the turn of the 19th century with the opening of Japan to tourism – had been reflected in other celebrated artists' gardens the principal being Monet's at Giverny. Broughton House garden is relatively small, at just under 0.5 hectare, and Japanese gardens are famed for their ingenious use of space. The garden incorporates the old gardens of 10 and 12 High Street and from 1908, that of number 14 which was purchased then. Hornel had first hand experience of Japan from visits made in 1893, with fellow artist, the Ayrshire painter George Henry, and later in 1920–21.

Hornel's purchase of Broughton House when he was under forty, was a sign of how successful his painting had become. He became less of a realist and more fanciful in his subjects, though trees, and wild and garden flowers (including snowdrops, wild roses, primroses and flax) were accurately depicted. At his death in 1933 he was a figure of the establishment. Broughton House itself contains Hornel pictures from the early and later periods and others, by friends such as George Henry, Bessie MacNicol and Jessie M. King. His collection of paintings, his large book collection and a recently discovered collection of photographs have been restored and are available for study, as the artist desired. His effects were preserved by a local Trust but after sixty years, the

E.A. Hornel and Elizabeth, his sister in the garden, a yucca behind them

upkeep had become too much to manage. The National Trust for Scotland took on the care of the property in 1997 and undertook renovation of house and garden. David Russell, gardener for the E.A. Hornel Trustees, was retained also by the Trust, preserving continuity until 2000 when Nick Hoskins became Head Gardener.

Some of Hornel's original planting survives: wisterias, tree paeonies and magnolia, for example. The focal point for the Japanese part of the garden is a double pool, the smaller part with stepping stones with a *faux* red-painted bridge, the larger surrounded by dwarf clipped box, dwarf rhododendrons, Japanese anemones, astilbes and other flowers. It is easy to forget that many valued staples in our gardens, such as skimmias *Skimmia japonica*, and the elegant variegated dogwood *Cornus controversa* 'Variegata', came from Japan. The cinnamon-barked, wall-trained lacecap hydrangea *Hydrangea anomala* subsp.

Rhododendron impeditum and *Anemonella thalictroides* growing in a stone trough

introduced plants. A golden false cypress *Chamae-cyparis pisifera* 'Filifera Aurea', is beautifully matched with the cascading foliage of a favourite plant from Japan: the golden grass *Hakonechloa macra* 'Aureola'. Elsewhere in the garden, Japanese cultivars have had preference. You can find the attractive hardy geranium *Geranium shikokianum*, and gentian *Gentiana triflora* var. *japonica*, and ferns, hostas and viburnums of Japanese origin.

While Hornel's original *Magnolia* x *soulangeana* looks splendid in its maturity, and the apple trees have roses decoratively growing over them, other plants such as the 13-metre high Lawson cypress, have grown out of proportion to the original design. Many of these mature trees and shrubs are in themselves objects of beauty so a continuous process of reassessment, co-ordination and adjustment has to take place.

The garden design consists of a symmetric arrangement of beds, lawns and borders, mostly edged in box. Here a larger palette of plants makes strong groupings and colour associations. The clipped balled hollies contrast with natural tree forms. The long border spills over with astilbes, the double blue hardy geranium *Geranium pratense* 'Plenum Violaceum', Dame's violet, dainty sidalceas, and tall hollyhocks, coming to a natural pause with a large elegant eucryphia. The garden is designed and planted so that each section leads into another without disclosing its secrets in advance.

The long main path runs along the line of the old garden boundary between the two old rigs of land amalgamated to make Broughton House garden in about 1813. The path structure on the Ordnance Survey map of 1894 looks similar to the current arrangement, so it seems that Hornel's design built on, and elaborated, an existing framework. Plants, especially the Japanese ones, grow well in the light,

petiolaris that covers the whole wall of the studio, another present-day favourite, is also Japanese.

The Japanese theme has been adroitly pursued into the present with the addition of more recently

▸ View through the 17th-century gate piers with *Cornus controversa* 'Variegata' and a sundial

fertile, slightly acid soil, With the estuary at its foot, the garden has a reliably mild climate, apart from sudden occasional frost and cold northwest winds.

Hornel collected sundials, placing five of them at significant points: centred within lawns, at path crossings or at the end of vistas. He liked the detail and texture of ancient stone, and he distributed a 12th-century granite cross, granite querns, troughs, millstones, and other stone artefacts and architectural fragments around the garden where they are artfully offset by plants. The evergreen trees and shrubs are offset by perennials, and annuals such as cosmos, nasturtiums, sweet Williams and old-fashioned snapdragons, with cool ferns and ivies and Japanese hostas in the shaded areas.

In keeping with the Japanese theme, the borders contain azaleas, hydrangeas and maples, with a handsome specimen of a mature paperbark maple *Acer griseum*, actually from China but grown in Japan and all over the temperate world. Rarer specimens include the white-flowered shrub *Clethra barbinervis*, and the graceful Japanese snowbell *Styrax japonicus* or the epaulette tree *Pterostyrax hispida*, which has aromatic grey bark and fragrant white flowers.

Snowdrops, like apple and pear blossom, were favourites of the artist that featured in his pictures. He built a small summer house, recently restored (though it no longer revolves to catch the sun as it used to). The small glasshouse where Hornel and his sister Elizabeth raised vegetables and ornamental plants is gone, but a fruit and vegetable plot is to be reinstated, for cultivars popular in the early 20th century. At the far end of the garden an intimate arbour, part of a raised platform looking out over the Dee, was Hornel's favourite spot.

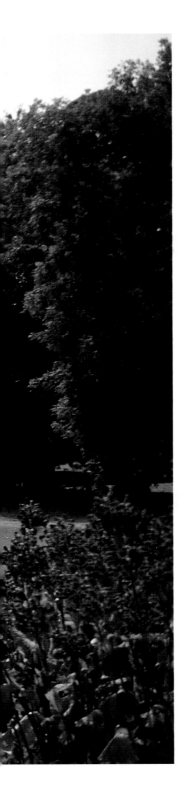

Castle Fraser

Beautiful individual trees, groves, avenues and sheltering woodlands surround the glowing cream structure of the castle, set in a gentle bowl of parkland in the valley of the River Don, northwest of Aberdeen. If you look down to Castle Fraser from the West Lodge (where the NE regional offices of The National Trust for Scotland are situated) it is like looking into a dreamy camera obscura, in which you watch the people around the castle, the trees, the birds and other animals below.

There was a hall on the site in 1454 when King James II granted Thomas Fraser this estate. In 1565 Michael Fraser began his new house, extending the original hall and adding, first, a round tower, then the square Michael tower. The castle itself is Scots baronial in style, with the grace of a French chateau, but fashioned in solid local granite Built with sturdy practicality but with grace and proportion, it

◀◀ Castle Fraser from the border outside the walled garden
◀ Part of the walled garden where the glasshouse range used to be

The castle in its grounds
by James Giles c.1850

Around this house, a spacious garden lies
Defended from the blasts of eastern skies
By thriving trees which to cast heights arise.
The best of fruits grow in this ferile ground
Well fenced with green enclosures all around.

allows itself some self-assured amusement in its ornamentation: the two pepperpot towers, the crowstepped gabling, the decorative cannon posing as gargoyles. These adornments were described as reflecting 'the richness of the Fraser estates combined with a desire to flaunt opulence'. Michael's son Andrew completed the square tower and built the flanking wings.

The strife of the Civil War impoverished the Frasers (some of whom were Covenanters, others Jacobites) and in 1644 the lands of Castle Fraser were laid waste. The Royalists 'spoilzeit his ground' and 'byrnt the ritche corne yairdes' but did little or no damage to the castle itself. How much the landscape recovered must be guessed, but a doggerel poem about the Don and its landscapes, attributed to Forbes of Brux in 1704 compliments the castle, 'raised with skill and art,/Magnificently built in every part.' As for the grounds:

The original landscape was moor and bog, but both lines of Frasers – and the Pearsons who were owners after them – and now The National Trust for Scotland, have been indefatigable tree-planters. Over the centuries the grounds were gradually drained, forested and coaxed into a landscape of fine woods and parkland. Roy's Military Survey of 1750 has three good-sized avenues of trees clearly marked. The records of the castle are full of items about trees, including orders for several hundred thousands at a time, and for individual specialities such as monkey puzzles. Comments on the state of the woods and park appear regularly. The sycamore avenue to the north is still impressive and those to the west and east exist, but less formally. Trees figure in all the maps and images of Castle Fraser. The estate has always been subject to wind damage. Large numbers of trees were lost in the 1953 gale and again in 2002, although the Broad Walk's northern avenue of sycamore survived.

Elyza Fraser, who succeeded to the estate in 1792, commissioned the landscape designer Thomas White (senior), the foremost exponent of the picturesque in Scotland, to improve the parkland. He and the owners fell out some time later but the first Ordnance Survey maps reveal that many of his proposals were adopted, others adapted to the Fraser taste, and some ignored. The three great avenues, marked for removal by White, were retained. However, clumps of trees were planted around the castle, in new areas of parkland and to

◀ Inside the walled garden, looking inwards to the centre

▼ The walled garden: the northeast corner and south-facing border, with wall fruit

▲ The old mill pond

▼ The avenue
to the castle with its
fine sycamores

form new woods such as Miss Bristow's Wood and
Alton Brae. White's serpentine lake southeast of the
castle was constructed, but never a success, was later
filled in. The ground remains boggy to this day.

Roy's 1750 survey, maps an enclosed area south
of the castle, probably a formal kitchen garden.
Survey maps of 1788, show considerable walled
gardens in three sections, directly to the east of the
castle, By about 1795, the walled garden is shown in
its current situation about 100 metres northeast of
the castle, with a surrounding envelope to the north
and east marked 'kitchen garden and orchard', and
shrubberies. It remains an impressive construction,
judiciously sited to catch the sun, with heat-holding
brick inner walls, 3.6 metres high. The external
north wall, which can be seen from the new east
avenue, is faced with granite. The first Ordnance
Survey map of 1856 shows the glasshouse in the
walled garden, a distinct yard to the east of the
garden, and the laundry and shrubbery further east.

In 1921, the castle was sold to the 1st Lord
Cowdray and given to his son, Clive Pearson, who
restored some of the garden. There are photographs of the walled garden from the 1920s, showing the large glasshouse, tidy rows of blackcurrant
bushes and herbaceous plants. A rose arbour surrounded the central water pump, and vegetables
filled beds on either side of axial path which was
flanked with antirrhinums. An RAF aerial photograph, taken in 1946, shows a neatly delineated
walled garden evidently in good working order,
with a large nursery area to its southeast, well sheltered by trees and shrubs. Clive's daughter, Lavinia
Smiley, and her husband, took a good deal of interest in the history and restoration of Castle Fraser.
They gave the castle and part of the parkland to
The National Trust for Scotland, which in 1993
purchased a further 130 hectares of the estate.

In the autumn of 2003, the Trust took out the
overgrown trees and shrubs and grass of the walled
garden, retaining the handsome flanking beech and
yew hedging. You can see the castle from within the
walled garden, and the box topiary around the rein-

stated ancient sundial of the central parterre is being clipped to the shape of the towers, to echo the flourish of the castle architecture. The original network of footpaths from 1795, has been uncovered, and four large island beds with trees, shrubs and perennials, created, each with its sitting area, so visitors can enjoy the scents and foliage textures. There is a border of medicinal and culinary herbs, traditional borders and wall-trained and soft fruit, and an organic vegetable garden.

The hot border against the south-facing wall flames impressively with tall eremurus lilies, Canna lilies, *Phygelius* x *rectus* 'African Queen', kniphofias, including the brilliant and long-lasting 'Sunningdale Yellow'. As you move into the walled garden, you are at once aware of the warmer microclimate and plants such as Chusan palm *Trachycarpus fortunei* and variably hardy salvias and *Lobelia tupa*, a startling 1.5 metres high, with downy grey-green leaves and bright crimson-maroon flower-spikes. Many half-hardy plants have survived thorugh recent mild winters, but temperatures can drop as low as -20⁰ Celsius.

Flowers contribute also to the landscape outside the walled garden. Along the south side of walled garden, and visible from the castle, is the restored Jim Russell border, designed for Mr and Mrs Smiley in 1959. It has been modified to accommodate plants suitable to the Aberdeenshire climate. The tree paeonies *Paeonia suffruticosa* 'Shou An Hong' and an interesting and unusual specimen of *Paeonia delavayi* are well worth the walk in early summer.

To the north of the walled garden, in contrast to its sunny openness, is a broad shady border lush with rodgersias, ligularia and the less common *Sinacalia tangutica*, which has yellow flowers and very cut leaves, blowsy *Filipendula camtschatica*, *Gunnera manicata*, hostas and the big *Geranium*

▲ The centrepiece of the walled garden with its sundial
▶ Looking through the beech hedge, screening part of the walled garden

palmatum. The most unusual plants in this border are *Kirengeshoma palmata* and *Podophyllum delavayi*. Nearby an attractive woodland garden (the shrubbery of two centuries earlier) has interesting plants all growing beautifully beneath some of the old tree planting including a wellingtonia from the 1850s and some recently planted cultivars of mountain ash *Sorbus aucuparia*. There are other podophyllums here looking wonderfully at home, and unusual primulas such as *Primula polyneura* with its palmate leaves and cerise flowers. These exotics merge with naturalised spring flowers such as winter aconite, snowdrops bluebells and hellebores. This is a garden of great charm and will be further developed to include a range of deciduous azaleas, and late-flowering rhododendrons. Rhododendrons were a favourite with Elyza Fraser.

Craigievar Castle

The castle at Craigievar gleams like a pale jewel set into its wooded hillside. The designed landscape owes its present beauty principally to its fine trees, set off by lawns, and pastures. The great conifers in the parkland near the castle are shapely and well spaced, almost as high as the castle whose architecture involves a flowing, expansive upper section rising from its tall straight towers. The castle sits on a plateau, looking southwest over the fertile valley, with thick, sheltering forest behind, its turrets and elegant ogee towers rising up among the parkland trees to the fore and sides.

This fine example of 17th-century Renaissance Scottish architecture; was built by William Forbes between 1610 and 1625, on the basis of an earlier castle. So skilfully was the incorporation achieved that the extent of the earlier building was only discovered when the pink harling (created out of the pink granite) was renewed in 1973. Craigievar combines the best of Scottish traditional style with the classical ornaments and symmetry of the Renaissance.

◀ The castle and the surviving part of the barmkin

The castle by James
Giles

No evidence survives of the earliest gardens although records make reference to a gardener there in 1696. Craigievar Castle and a simple outline of enclosed parks to the west appear in Roy's map of about 1750. The woods planted up the hill were shown at this time. In 1776, William Forbes, the 5th Earl, commissioned George Brown, who worked later at Leith Hall, to make a survey of the Craigievar policies. His map shows an enclosed garden divided into four to the north of the castle and a garden with trees to the east and south. A geophysical survey of this site has shown evidence of former paths, trenches and planting pits within this old enclosed garden.

Part of an older courtyard enclosure or barmkin with a turretted tower makes an interesting counterpoint to the present entrance. The rough stone of the wall, with a massive doorway, is dotted with ferns on the shady side and small flowering plants such as toadflax and fairy foxglove *Erinus alpinus* on the other. Up above the barmkin lie a small group of buildings that appear first in a map from the time of the 7th Baronet, John Forbes, as offices and a stackyard. The dwellings are now used by the Trust for staff and holiday visitors. Adjacent is a small garden supplying soft fruit and flowers for the castle which should be open to the public before long.

Various improvements were made to the castle interior, particularly by Sir John Forbes, who in 1824 commissioned a report on the state of the castle from the Aberdeen architect and builder John Smith. The recommended repairs: repainting, reproofing and reharling were carried out to the highest standards and more windows were put in. The intention was to preserve the historic aspect of the castle, while creating a comfortable and `commodious residence for the summer months'. A painting of the hall at Craigievar by James Skene of Rubislaw was used to illustrate Sir Walter Scott's novel *Redgauntlet*.

The formal elements of the castle landscape were swept away in the 19th century. In 1800, the great avenue of beeches to the south was planted, impressively lining what was then the main entrance drive. Most of the barmkin was taken down. The north block is still evident in a survey of 1819, in contrast to the clear view of the castle shown in depictions two or three decades later. A ha-ha was made to open up the view of the surrounding country. A watercolour by James Giles, the artist and landscape designer, in 1840 shows the castle to advantage in its parkland setting, the view unimpeded by its former enclosures or orchards. It is possible that the artist (who was also a practical landscape designer) was responsible for the alterations, but at present this is conjecture.

Old-fashioned practices such as strewing the floor with rushes freshly cut from the area below the castle, near the burn, were continued up into the mid-19th century, in affectionate deference to a traditional Scottish way of life. The respect for the castle's past history that had come naturally to the Forbes family, had by the mid 19th-century, become fashionably romantic. Craigievar, in Sir Andrew Leith-Hay's influential 1849 volume *Aberdeenshire Castles* was 'the beau ideal interior of a castle of olden time'. The surrounding landscape with its beautiful trees and open views was equally fashionable.

Craigievar became popular with celebrity tourists, including Queen Victoria, who paid two visits, and by her own account greatly enjoyed them. The family (who changed their name to Forbes-Sempill and then Sempill) used it more, and the style of repairs and improvements became more consciously Scottish-Baronial revivalist. By 1914, after the wartime requisition of their main family home Fintray, near Aberdeen, the 18th Lord Sempill and his wife decided to make Craigievar their principle abode, and in 1962 Lady Sempill opened negotiations with The National Trust for Scotland in order to preserve this important property, and the castle and 13 hectares, passed to the Trust a year later. In 2004, the Trust purchased a further 84 hectares of woodland.

At present, the approach to the castle, takes you through an attractive strip of oak woodland, so the castle is hidden from view until you walk up the path. Although the south drive is now out of use, it makes a pleasant walk with primroses, wood anemones, bluebells and other wild flowers on the banks, plentiful birdsong, and views over the valley. The old beeches that line the avenue are still magnificent though showing signs of age. The walk back to the castle makes a graceful uphill swirl that takes you past a wild-flower bank with star of Bethlehem and primroses, edging a rectangle of lawn that used to be a bowling green. Walks to the west, further up the hill reveal an 18th-century ring enclosure.

The lawns sloping away from the castle were planted with conifers later in the 19th century. There are several tall wellingtonias *Sequoiadendron giganteum* a beautifully proportioned monkey puzzle *Araucaria araucana* and two superb silver firs (*Abies alba*) that overtop the wellingtonias, one of them

reaching 43 metres. A fine old laburnum makes a dazzling display to the south in the springtime and presents a living knot of contorted trunks and branching through the winter. There have been subsequent plantings, a group of pale-leaved whitebeams on the sloping lawn, for example, that brighten the route to the south.

The area to the north of the outbuildings was labelled on the 1776 survey as the cornyard. It is now heavily shaded with trees growing around and over it, and it is full of mossy rocks that seem to be the remains of a rocky garden cut by a small ravine. It had been known as 'the Japanese garden' probably because of the Japanese maples in it, but the original was a Scottish glen garden, designed in the 1930s and described as having been planted with purple heather. The Trust plans to recreate this glen garden as far as is possible, given the shading from the trees in and around it.

The castle in its parkland setting with its fine trees

Crarae

The garden at Crarae lies within about 40 hectares of woods, much of it planted around the Crarae Burn which runs between small gorges, tumbling over rocks to the sea. The woodland, planted over centuries with its increments of exotic plants from the Indian subcontinent, China and Australasia, is acknowledged as a masterpiece. Roy Lancaster described the burn garden at Crarae as 'the nearest thing in Britain to a Himalayan gorge'. In 2002 The National Trust for Scotland, took over ownership (from the Crarae Garden Charitable Trust) with the purpose of restoring its historic significance, reopening paths and bridges – and also to develop the garden.

Crarae has a significant collection of rhododendrons and other choice plants of temperate forests, but the guiding motive has always been to create a garden rather than to assemble plant collections. A formidable number of eminent gardeners are believed to have contributed ideas and plants. The

◀◀ Looking out over Loch Fyne to the Cowal Hills
◀ Sweet-scented azaleas on one of the woodland paths

43

The mainspring of the garden at Crarae has always been good planting, but the terrain itself — one of the most beautiful parts of Argyll — has a natural charm. It attracted people in Neolithic times and part of a prehistoric chambered cairn to the west of the burn, bears testimony to their presence. There is, to this day, a stillness around the stone slabs of this well-preserved monument. A high proportion of natural woodland characterises this region, augmented by planting, which, at Crarae, began in the early 1800s.

From the mid-13th century, the estate had been part of the Lordship of Glassary, encompassing land between Loch Awe and Loch Fyne. The natural woodland passed though several hands before, in 1799, coming into the possession of Crawford Tait to whom, it is believed, the garden owes the fine European larch, and the Scots pine in the glen. Tait's brother-in-law, Sir Archibald Campbell of Succoth, bought the estate from him in 1825 but it was visited infrequently until, in 1893, Margaret, Lady Campbell pulled down the inn known as Crarae, rebuilt the house as we see it today (where Sir Ilay and the present Lady Campbell live and not open to the public). She made a rock garden of some of the rubble from the demolition and planted conifers, which may be ancestors of the Lawson cypresses in the garden.

Margaret's husband's cousin, Sir Archibald the 5th Baronet succeeded to the family properties in 1909. His wife Grace, a keen gardener, was aunt to Reginald Farrer whose plant-finding expeditions to Gansu and Upper Burma provided many plants for gardens worldwide. The rock garden that Grace developed, has disappeared, but several large conifers still grow on the natural outcrop to the northwest of the house where it was situated. Most of Margaret's Crarae planting was around

The Waterfall Bridge over the Crarae Burn with self-sown rhododendrons, birch and cotoneasters amongst the original planting

Campbells of Stonefield, pioneers of wild gardening in Argyll, and Sir John Maxwell of Pollok (a founder of The National Trust for Scotland), are thought to have had considerable influence and to have contributed plants, as did Mairi Sawyer of Inverewe, the Balfours of Dawyck, the Royal Botanic Garden Edinburgh, Lord Strathcona of Colonsay, and Sir James Horlick of Gigha.

the house, with shrub borders of some distinction.

The rhododendrons she introduced to the west of the burn were planted under the shelter of Crawford Tait's now mature and beautiful larches. Her large cream-flowered *Rhododendron falconeri* still flowers each spring from this planting, which was augmented skilfully by her son, Sir George Campbell, the creative genius of Crarae, who took over the estate in 1925. An early interest in trees led him, as a child, to plant a giant fir *Abies grandis* (now a fine tree) and a few years later to adopt an unwanted Chinese fir, *Cunninghamia lanceolata*, from Dawyck – which flourished alongside his mother's *Rhododendron falconeri*.

He continued, with remarkable success, to plant unusual trees, including the elegant Korean pine *Pinus koraiensis*, and the Korean fir *Abies koreana*, *Saxegothaea conspicua*, a tender tree with leaves a little like yew, and the North American mountain hemlock, *Tsuga mertensiana*. He had an extraordinary talent for placing trees and shrubs in happy combination, so that they thrived to produce a beautiful and naturalistic landscape. From the high path by the waterfall, you look over native trees, such as birch, oak, alder, rowan and hazel, interspersed with maples, stuartias and fothergillas. Everything grows so well; there are cotoneasters that are large trees. Rhododendrons are also part of the vista: from the early golden bloom of *Rhododendron lutescens*, to the late flowering 'Tally Ho' with its red blossom. Sir George increased the rhododendrons, often choosing hybrids that would flourish at Crarae rather than rare species. He was unusual in recognising the qualities of some of the best self-sown hybrids: the creamy white-flowered *Rhododendron wardii* individuals with purple blotched blooms, for example. He raised a superb *Rhododendron lacteum* x *R. maccabeanum* hybrid

▲ A May-flowering rhododendron of the *Triflora* subsection with bluebells and azaleas

▶ This handsome lupin clump (at the bottom bridge in a private area of Sir Ilay's garden) has reverted to blue from a multi-coloured Russell lupin planting many years ago

45

The prehistoric cist burial chamber and a fine *Rhododendron* 'Loder's White'

(now known as *Rhododendron* 'Rohais' after the present Lady Campbell) from seed from the Royal Botanic Garden, Edinburgh. On the higher slopes to the west, part of the garden was devoted to raising hybrid seed bred by a neighbour, Lord Glenkinglas. Some of the successes are still flowering.

Sir George had a wide range of interests that included trees from temperate forests such as the Chilean firebush *Embothrium coccineum*, shrubs such as *Styrax* species, white-flowering eucryphias, magnolias, the evergreen *Trochodendron aralioides* with its spiral leaves, and the southern beech *Nothofagus*, of which Crarae is a National Plant Collection holder.

One of the main paths leads through eucalyptus in a large grove that looks almost prehistoric, especially in misty conditions. Sir George planted twenty species, mostly from Tasmania. Beyond this, the path leads out of the trees to an open track with views of Loch Fyne. The Trust has marked traditional routes through the garden, some short and easy, others longer and more strenuous, but this is only the beginning of the rediscovery – there is much more to explore and develop in the recesses of this magical woodland.

It is still early days at Crarae for The National Trust for Scotland, which has already done a lot a repair work on paths and bridges. Much research is needed to identify plants and to establish the present state of the plant collection, and how it may best be conserved and developed in the context of the special distinctiveness of this much-loved garden.

I was fortunate to be at Crarae early in August 2004 in conditions that occur, perhaps, once in a lifetime. The woodland was full and leafy in its lush greens, lit here and there with late summer bloom, but instead of a gentle summer trickle, the burn was a torrent, swollen by the extreme rainfall of the previous days. At the waterfall bridge, the noise and spray was stupendous. The mass of water was so great that part of its flow had leapt out of the streambed tearing though the trees and over the path, to join the mainstream further down the waterfall. It was exhilerating experience. The water at this high point in the garden resumed its normal route after a few hours, without damage to the upper path, but downsteam, part of a burnside path just opened, was swept away and the banks on both sides scoured clean down to the gleaming grey boulder clay. This path has been reinstated so visitors can again follow this route to the heart of the garden and enjoy the burn in its quieter moods.

An abundance of plants growing together has always been characteristic of Crarae: exotics such as rhododendron and Japanese maple mingle with native and naturalised birches, and native oak and bluebells

Crathes Castle

▲ A lovely clump of Lady fern *Athyrium filix-femina* in the Upper Pool garden

◀ The root network of a fine beech growing up the cliff in Caroline's Garden

The castle and its large walled garden are the two most famous elements within the landscape of Crathes Castle. This large (215 hectare) estate in its beautiful and sheltered situation above the River Dee, looks over to the Grampians and into Angus. It had been in the continuous possession of the Burnett family until it came to the Trust in 1951. For nearly 400 years Crathes has developed incrementally from a 'craggy hillside' to a complex and remarkable designed landscape. I would advise a visitor to take the time to enjoy the sense of place and to explore the balancing elements: the architecture, the enclosed garden, expansive sloping lawns, bordered by woods, the remarkable cliffside garden and the wider park and woodland with their fine trees.

The Burnett family themselves might be considered almost a part of this landscape, for they had lived nearby even before they built Crathes Castle. Alexander and Janet Burnett began the castle in the last quarter of the 16th century, and it was finished by their great-grandson, (also Alexander), who moved to the new castle in the early years of the 17th century. The impressive building of rough

49

granite covered with harling, with its playful round towers and turrets, was the work of an Aberdeen family of master masons named Bel. The Queen Anne wing to the east of the original castle was damaged by fire twice in the 20th century and partly restored. It gives a view out on to the Upper Pool Garden, designed by Lady Sybil Burnett in the early 20th century, which retains her striking and innovative Mediterranean-like tonal scheme of brilliant red, gold and orange, against a background of bronze and purple.

Early references indicate that the castle had trees and gardens shortly after it was built. Robert Gordon of Straloch in 1640 noted much tree planting and that Alexander's son Thomas Burnett (the 1st Baronet) 'has covered the forbidding crags, laid it out with gardens and dotted it with pleasaunce'. The walled garden, close to the castle occupies part of the hill facing southeast. The trees protected it from the winds and, then as now, the walled garden had a gentle, mild microclimate, unusual for a situation so far northeast and 350ft above sea-level. In 1714, Sir Samuel Forbes of Foveran remarked on the warmth of the soil and 'delicate fruit' of the Crathes gardens, and nearly a century later the author of *The Agricultural Survey of Kincardineshire* (G. Robertson) exclaimed he had 'nowhere else in Scotland met with such a profusion of fruits as in these gardens'. Gradually these superb kitchen gardens became pleasure gardens, and the planting purely ornamental.

Nothing prepares you for the present beauty within the walled garden as you approach the little entrance over the wide lawn. The first sense of what is to come is glimpsed through Robert

◀ Steps to the Aviary Terrace and the upper garden with the castle beyond

Hutchison's modern gate in wrought iron, installed in the 1980s to recall the 'Wrot Iron gate' made by a Glasgow firm of iron workers in 1850s. Inside, the abundance of plants is almost oppressive: enticing perimeter paths of blue and pink to the north, golden through the rose arch to the south, while ahead the white border, with its well-known *Philadelphus* collection, beckons. There is a fine *Philadelphus* 'Beauclerk' and the exceptionally fragrant Crathes form of *P. purpurascens* whose purplish outer sepals tone subtly with the purple hedging of *Prunus cerasifera* 'Pissardii' that backs the white border. A superb Portugal laurel *Prunus lusitanica*, clipped into a neat mushroom with a seat beneath, at the end of this border marks the central crossing point of the lower garden.

Looking over the lower garden from the Aviary Terrace to the Grampians beyond

Trimming part of the castle's vast yew hedges in the blue-themed Fountain Garden

The impact of this garden with its double levels depends principally on well-grown plants in happy association. The simple divisions of early kitchen gardens are retained, with a peripheral path and quartering paths. Diversion for the eye is provided by the different levels, and outward views from each section.

From the double border that runs north from the laurel, extends a view to the famous ancient yews of the upper garden, with a glimpse of the castle beyond. Looking in reverse, south from the higher level of the Aviary Terrace, you can see the double border with its adjacent Camel Garden and Trough Garden, and to the open countryside with the Grampians beyond. It is a stunning view, but it comes at a price. The clearance of the sheltering trees to the south, cut in the mid-1800s to create

this vista, allows winds into the garden. When conditions are exactly at their worst, a chilling southeasterly can sweep off the hills and over the garden, blasting the plants. In 1995, when this occurred, even the buddlejas were killed. The early springs prevalent nowadays bring a new problem, when early sappy growth coincides with winds that can suddenly turn chill and blacken the new shoots.

Gold-themed gardens are too often unpleasantly brash, but I advise you not to miss the Golden Garden that occupies the lower southwest quarter of the walled garden. It dates from 1973, but it was always the intention of Lady Burnett to develop a golden theme. To make it, the Trust drew on the forty years of knowledge and practical skills of the then Head Gardener Douglas MacDonald and

▶ The spring early summer garden, the doocot enclosure, with it show of trilliums

Frances Chenevix Trench who also contributed much to the garden, the White Border, in particular.

The distinctiveness of this area derives, as elsewhere, from choice of plant, and placing each to associate excitingly with its companions. Tulip, 'Golden Apeldoorn', golden periwinkle and Bowles golden grass are interwoven with shrubs such as the golden currant *Ribes sanguineum* 'Brocklebankii' and *Berberis thunbergii* 'Aurea' and spiraea and the unusual yellow-flowered *Weigela middendorffiana*. Blooms of *Inula magnifica* reach two metres or more whilst the tiny flowers of *Hacquetia epipactis* and sprawling *Lysimachia nummularia* 'Aurea' snuggle diminuitively into border fronts beside glowing euphorbias.

The glasshouses to the north of the lower garden were restored in the 1970s and are again in use for growing flowers and displays for the castle. These glasshouses were famous for their wall-trained zonal pelagoniums, grown as cut flowers. The idea for growing them in this way was adopted by Douglas MacDonald, Head Gardener from 1951 to 1992.

In the magnificent June Borders to the south, the eye is drawn to the attractive doocot (moved to this position in 1937) These borders were created by Lady Burnett in 1945 and contain old-fashioned cottage garden flowers, at their peak in midsummer: poppies, lupins, salvias and pyrethrums, and a star turn in rich blue from the Caucasus, the goat's rue *Galega orientalis*. Tall cirsiums and over twenty different rose paeonies add to the richness. Most of these are propagated from the very fine forms picked out by Lady Burnett in the first half of the 20th century, many of them no longer available.

There are, for example, four different forms of the tall thistle *Cirsium rivulare* and a form of the fragrant Sichuan *Iris chrysographes* that is almost black.

Each of the eight sections of the whole walled garden is distinct and filled with very fine plants. Lady Burnett had a superb eye for a good plant and an ability to pick out the best forms, and cultivars and Callum Pirnie, the present Head Gardener, has found it preferable, in terms of quality as well as of historical authenticity, to propagate from the plants in the garden rather than to buy in when the plants need replacing. However, the health of certain plants has deteriorated over the years. The giant lilies *Cardiocrinum giganteum* that grow to 3 metres, and its variety *C. g.* var. *yunnanense*, were coming up smaller and smaller over the decades, and have

A grumpy stone image on the old sundial

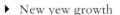
▲ The dramatic cutting back of the south side of the yew hedge

▶ New yew growth

Great yews divide the upper and lower levels of the walled garden. Old engravings have shown that there had been eight ancient topiary yews, probably dating from about 1700, and that the infilling hedges, which used to include holly but are now all yew are a later addition. The base for one of these old yews was identified during recent cutting back and it is being restored to its former shape. The yews have always been clipped, but even so, over centuries of growth, they were becoming so much out of proportion with the other parts of the garden that it was decided to cut them hard back. An operation such as this on trees of great historic importance, and immense significance within the garden requires patience and good preparation. First, the hedge and its topiaries are brought into peak condition, then the south-facing side is cut back to the wood. The slower-growing northern side will not be cut. This procedure seems to be successful and in a few years the rejuvenated yews are again growing strongly, and the normal annual clipping can be resumed.

The Upper Garden, reached by means of some balustraded stairs and quartered like the lower half, has been the main pleasure garden since the early 1800s. The main living quarters of Sir and Lady Sybil were enlivened by a view out to the Upper Pool Garden where a succession of rich colours played against each other through the year but never more so than in the late summer into early autumn. Gorgeous helianthemums in yellow, red, and bronze, flare alongside select crocosmias such as bronze-leaved 'Solfatare' and the coppery-apricot 'Jenny Bloom'. *Kniphofia caulescens* blooms late, lasting almost to November, its grey-blue evergreen foliage shows up the coral-coloured flower-heads. The statuesque plants extend along into the Croquet Lawn and link the two gardens.

been replaced with magnificent bulbs wild collected from the Himalayas at the turn of the millennium. There is at present a careful strategy of replacement of plants taking place throughout the lower walled garden.

The bright flower colours and the foliage purples and bronzes, change with the light and with the seasons in a masterly planting orchestration. The Upper Pool Garden was Lady Burnett's last garden work and arguably her boldest and best. She could enjoy the effects from her sitting room which was part of the Victorian extension. This was not rebuilt after the fire but visitors today can look down from a patio built on the level of the first floor drawing room.

Beyond lies the Fountain Garden, which the Burnetts maintained in its Victorian style with bedding plants such as the old fashioned Chinese forget-me-not *Cynoglossum amabile* grown in 1928, and intensely blue Salvia patens in formal beds. Its blue theme continues, but annuals such love-in- the- mist, bedding cultivars of viper's bugloss *Echium vulgare* 'Blue Bedder', *Anchusa capensis* 'Blue Angel', are now direct sown into the box-edged beds. The three clipped Portugal laurels, holly and fastigiate yews to the east of garden, mirror those in the adjacent Rose Garden. The fountain sculpture, a copy of one that once stood in the Palazzo Vecchio in Florence gives a subtle link to the Italianate Pool Garden. The Rose Garden, with its pink, red and white floribunda beds, edged in 'Hidcote' lavender, was designed by Lady Burnett in 1946. The old lawn of the Croquet Lawn, which makes the fourth quarter of the upper level, features on a map of 1798, but it was adapted for croquet some time after the game was invented in the mid-19th century.

The outer borders of the upper and lower gardens contain many rare and unusual trees and

▲ The golden garden with the golden maple *Acer cappadocicum* 'Aureum'

◀ The Fountain Garden looking over the echium

▶ The wild cliff garden (Caroline's Garden) with shuttlecock ferns unfolding and coppiced Amur maple *Acer tataricum* subsp. *ginnala*

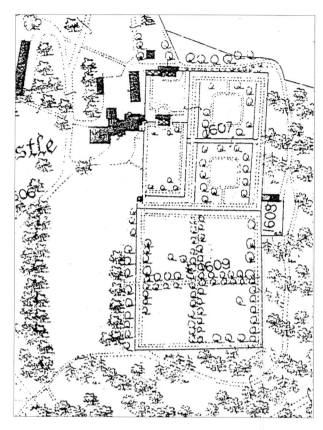

Crathes Castle and gardens as they appeared on the 1864 and 1901 1:2500 OS Maps

The old laburnum lights up the path down to the walled garden

shrubs collected by Sir James Burnett, including a multi-stemmed pocket handkerchief tree *Davidia involucrata*. Some of these plants have become too large and are being propagated and replanted. Sir James extended the collection to the south into the quiet woodland garden and into the surrounding woods where there are some magnificent specimen trees, all the more remarkable when the thin, rocky soil is taken into account. Planting here is better achieved with a crowbar than a spade, and in most places the rock lies just below the surface.

Across the lawns to the west of the walled garden lie lovely woodlands. Some of the trees are native. Others, including many unusual kinds, were purchased by Sir James, (a considerable number from his old friend Sir Harold Hillier). They were planted both for their individual beauty and for the shelter they provided. He planted a wide selection of southern beech, *Nothofagus* species some of which are now splendid in maturity, and many exceptional firs including an *Abies spectabilis* var.

brevifolia. One of the rarest specimens, a small miracle for the northeast, is *Taiwania cryptomerioides* just above the castle, a tree with beautiful and unusual foliage with needles and compound leaves. Many generations of Burnetts, including his own father, had taken had a great interest in trees and planting on the estate, so Sir James – and subsequently, the Trust – had a good basis on which to build. There is a hilly part to the west where the rocks, though mossy and laced with plants, give the distinct impression of having been arranged. It is possible that these were rocks excavated when the walled garden was made. This

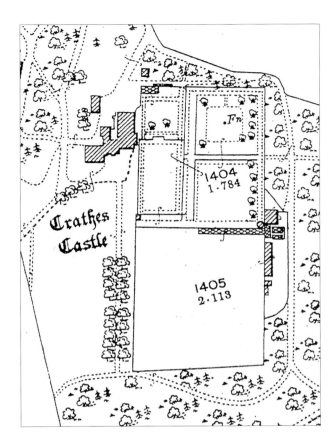

hillock may have been part of a craggy woodland garden.

Just to the north, a path leads to what is now known as Caroline's Garden, which is a wild garden beneath a granite cliff (restored by The National Trust for Scotland's Conservation Volunteers). Native and naturalised trees and shrubs grow together in a dramatic setting that includes meadow, wetland and vertical granite cliff. Directly under the cliff is a magnificent beech, Scots pines grow higher up, and a few rhododendrons have been planted in crevices. In the sunny, humid shelter below, there are naturalised azaleas, Himalayan primroses, and an unusual and very graceful mounded honey-suckle *Lonicera syringantha* which has bell-like,

fragrant pink flowers. The *Eucryphia* x *nymanensis* 'Nymansay' has become a remarkable tree about 15 metres high. Many of the plants are only doubt-fully hardy so far north, but in this sheltered micro-climate, even the Japanese umbrella pine, *Sciadopitys verticillata* has survived and reached a height of 6 metres.

Unusual trees extend into the surrounding estate, which invites walkers to explore its woodland trails. There is abundant wildlife: wild flowers, birds such as woodpeckers goldcrests, treecreepers, and squirrels and deer and other mammals. By the lakes and the Burn of Coy, live otters, herons, duck and other water birds. Crathes combines the natural and exotic within a judicious and skilfully designed landscape, and in this lies its delight.

Looking along the double herbaceous border towards the glasshouse

Culross Palace

From the hillside of the ancient seaport village of Culross on the north bank of the Firth of Forth with its 16th- and 17th-century buildings in their glowing saffron-gold harling, you can dimly see the distant chimneys and superstructures of modern industry across the river. In its heyday the Royal Burgh of Culross was a busy and important port, with international trade, principally coal and salt with the Netherlands and Baltic states. Now, in the 21st century, it is again thriving, as people return to see the beautifully conserved town restored to a high standard by The National Trust for Scotland and Historic Scotland.

Two of the most important buildings owned by the Trust, are the Town House, overlooking the sea, an old Customs House that is now used for exhibitions, and Culross Palace which was built by Sir George Bruce between 1597 and 1611. The fabric of Culross Palace is evidence of Bruce's standing and success in foreign trade. Most of the building materials – Dutch

◀◀ Looking over the garden to the palace, the Firth of Forth beyond and ◀ Greens in the vegetable garden

The great flowerhead of globe artichoke 'Purple Globe'

▶ Looking westwards across the vegetable garden on the middle terrace: the curry plant *Helichrysum* around the leeks, purple sage and lavender bordering the other beds

▶▶ Three wall-trained pears backing the herb bed

allows Mediterranean herbs to flourish, the tender rabbit-eared *Lavandula stoechas* alongside rosemary, lovage, fennel, savory, rue and the curry plant *Helichrysum italicum*. Sage is used as well as lavender to edge some of the beds and borders.

When the garden was begun in 1993, it was one of the Trust's most exciting developments, a forerunner of recreated historic gardens with period plants. There are now many such gardens, but this pioneer has developed into a productive and attractive maturity, the fruit and vegetables from its raised beds supplying the tea room on the lower ground floor of Bessie Bar Hall adjacent to the palace.

The middle terrace includes many plants used for physic as well as for culinary and decorative purposes. The scented pinks, foxglove, *Scrophularia nodosa*, hellebore and goat's-rue are included here. A lemon-yellow wolf's-bane *Aconitum lycoctonum*, tall orange-yellow *Inula helenium* and bright St John's wort make a historical statement into vivid ornament. Old cornfield weeds, some now quite rare, such as white campion, corn marigold, corncockle and cornflower, are grown in the herb beds at the back of the vegetable garden. Fan and espalier apples, pears and cherries share the high terrace walls with jasmine and roses.

Hollyhocks blaze like red and pink flags when you look up from the lower garden. The taller herbs and vegetables such as lovage and globe artichoke also link the different levels of the garden. The late medieval method of growing herbs and vegetables in geometric raised beds is attractive as well as productive. The garden is busy though not large, and there is always something to catch the eye. The criss-cross paths are surfaced with shells from the beach, crushed and raked flat.

The beds at Culross brim with produce. The vegetables are often companioned by flowering plants

floor tiles and glass, pine from the Baltic, red pantiles from the Low Countries – were brought to Culross as ballast in his trading ships. The building, with its beautiful painted wooden ceilings, was restored in 1996 and the Trust reconstructed a period garden up the steep, south-facing hillside behind the palace. A terraced garden of fruit, flowers and vegetables extends over the main central area, with a orchard to one side with Scots Dumpy chickens, one of the oldest known breeds, known in Scotland nine centuries ago, and possibly originating further back in time.

From the highest point in the garden looking above the lavender-edged walk, with hollyhocks and roses, and the counterpane of fruits, herbs and vegetables, you have one of the best views possible over the town and the old harbour (one of the oldest in Scotland) and across the Firth. The stone soaks up the summer heat, and on a hot day the colours are dazzling, and you are grateful for the shelter of a covered mediaeval seat, with its apron of cool grassy lawn, and the shade of the black mulberry and vine allée. The warmth

such as marigolds and poppies growing alongside them. There is an asparagus bed, and gooseberry bushes, neat blocks of leeks, and handsome cabbages. Parsnips and cabbages are protected from flies by an open-weave netting. There are also some unusual crops such as purple-flowered broad beans and asparagus pea with its little winking red flowers.

On the shadier walls, there are ferns and wall plants and there are wicker baskets boxes with ferns in them. The whole effect is crisp and well-cared for. From the garden you hear the sounds of both seabirds and garden songbirds. Robins are especially appropriate as they are the birds of St Kentigern (also known as St Mungo) the patron saint of Glasgow, who was born and brought up at Culross in the 6th century.

Culzean Castle

Culzean Castle crouches on top of the cliffs, looking out to sea over the Firth of Clyde on one side and over its historic gardens and policies on the other, a splendid backdrop for the extensive gardens. The Culzean Kennedys were the moving force in the Carrick region of Ayrshire for five centuries, but it was two brothers, Thomas and David Kennedy, the 9th and 10th Earls of Cassillis, who developed and augmented the castle and gardens as we know them today, with further improvements, especially to the estate, made by the 12th Earl, also Archibald Kennedy who was created the 1st Marquess of Ailsa. The great castle designed by Robert Adam for David Kennedy, the 10th Earl, between 1777 and 1792, was constructed over previous dwellings and fortifications that date back to 1270.

The bones of Culzean's history underlie what we see today. The bank along the south end of the fountain garden beneath the terraced walks marks

◀ This painting of Culzean from the southeast, attributed to Robert Adam after the first stage of his alterations, hangs in the castle

the remains of the old coal road. Artefacts from the 18th and 19th centuries that have been covered over and forgotten are being recovered in the course of restoration work. It was discovered that Culzean had a substantial icehouse, built deep into the walls below the Adam bridge within the viaduct, and in 1999 an amazingly intact, complex system of underground heating and ventilation was uncovered during archaeological work that took place while restoring the glasshouses. The Trust is also considering the reconstruction of vistas that recreate the qualities of surprise and sense of movement, so integral to the picturesque ideal. The picturesque landscape design substantially developed by the 12th Earl, but overgrown, is being disclosed through clearing, and the restoration of ruined early 19th-century buildings such as the Pagoda and Camellia House.

Arriving at Culzean in March from the chilly southern counties of England, I was surprised to hear the singing of the first migrant chiffchaffs of spring, and to find smiling warm terraces and the woodland gardens brimming with blossom, daffodils and other spring flowers. This part of coastal South Ayrshire is sheltered, humid and mild, warmed by the North Atlantic Drift. Here many warm-climate plants can flourish outdoors: tree ferns *Dicksonia antarctica*, tree-like cordylines, 2-metre-high Madeiran and Canary Island echiums, and numerous tender bulbs and herbaceous plants.

The beautifully kept walled garden at a little distance from the castle has a grand entrance gate designed by Robert Adam and dated 1786. To hold the warmth, the outside is built of sandstone and the inner skin is of brick. It is a double-plan walled garden, divided in two by a glorious suite of restored glasshouses. The northern half, the 'engine room' of the working garden, contains the fruit trees and bushes and the cut flower beds and borders. Nowadays it runs on much the same lines but on a smaller scale. Fruit and flowers are still sent up to the castle, but to the restaurant rather than the family table. Plants are trialled and cuttings lined out to make new plants. Plants for sale are propagated here. Wide and dramatic borders line the cross paths, centred on an unusual sundial with 52 facets, and a collection of kniphofia is being built up.

The flowers for the castle are generally old favourites: Dame's violet *Hesperis matrionalis* tulips of various kinds, honesty, irises, alchemillas, sweet William, delphiniums, stocks and statice, with gladioli, dahlias and chrysanthemums going through to the end of the season. The soil in this garden is workable and fertile with good drainage and a neutral pH. Horse manure is still added, the current practice of using sawdust rather than straw bedding making it easier to work. As with most Trust gardens, the staff here use pesticides only when absolutely necessary.

The grassy orchard is especially productive in cooking apples, and on the surrounding walls, new fruit trees are bring trained. Currants of various kinds and raspberries grow in extensive fruit cages. The most spectacular wall fruit is undoubtedly a fig tree on the south-facing wall in the next door half of the garden; it is reckoned to be 160 years old, and has, over time, layered itself a distance of 25 metres.

Fruit is also to be found in the herb garden made in 1991, just outside the walls, which is bisected by a fruit arch of Scottish apples such as 'Galloway Pippin', 'Stirling Castle', 'Seaton House' and 'Lady of the Wemyss'.

The southern half of the walled garden has always been a place to display the skill and enterprise of the gardeners. The glasshouses restored inside and out to the perfection of their late Victorian predecessors, include a conservatory with seasonal displays of orchids – especially cymbidiums – pelargoniums, geraniums and begonias. The specialist houses nurture beautifully pruned peaches, nectarines, apricots and vines, representing the best range of indoor fruit in the Trust. The Head Gardener, Susan Russell, has tracked down and replanted late 19th-century grape varieties, which, with skilled care, are growing strongly.

The beds in front of the peach house demonstrate how surprisingly many plants, manage to overwinter in this gentle climate, good soil and favoured position. Cistus, osteospermums, diascias and nemesias regularly overwinter. If there are

◀◀ A detail of the walled garden herbaceous border with the head gardener's house beyond.

▼ A walk by the borders in the middle terrace in front of the castle

losses, it is usually owing to wet rather than cold, but since cuttings are taken anyway, this is usually not serious. The other long bed by the glasshouses contains a varied of bulbs: the strongly scented acidanthera, colourful tigridia and hemerocallis together with spiky phormiums and agaves. Many of the plants in this monocot border would not be regarded as hardy in Britain, but overwinter happily here. There are a number of watsonias and a crocosmia variety *Crocosmia pottsii* 'Culzean Peach'.

A vast and aged *Rhododendron ponticum* used to sprawl near to the entrance of the walled garden, now replaced by a formal round arbour of high beech hedges designed to be clipped to 2 metres with a 3-metre centrepiece of pleached hornbeam. The hedge will have a window cut out of it, to provide a view beyond to the great cedar of Lebanon and the sandstone grotto. The orange-brown, iron-rich sandstone of the grotto, built in the early 1900s, glows warm, even in the winter months. Originally planted with ivy and ferns, it is now covered with the blooms of rock plants from spring until late autumn, providing a pleasant view from the restored thatched tea house.

The southerly point of the walled garden, rejoices in a boisterous spiral border planted with a jungle of large damp loving plants with big leaves: gunneras, *Rheum palmatum* 'Atrosanguineum' *Rodgersia aesculifolia*, and ligularias *Ligularia przewalskii* and *L. dentata*, royal fern, and fan palm *Trachycarpus fortunei*. There are banana plants *Musa basjoo*, here, closely bandaged with windbreak polythene during the winter months and unfurling their huge leaves for the summer.

Many special trees and shrubs lie on the hillside leading to the restored Camellia House, an elegant building designed in 1818 by James Donaldson (a pupil of Robert Adam) as an orangery, and reopened in 1996. The pink flowers of the magnolia *Magnolia campbellii* subsp. *mollicomata* and huge early-flowering tree rhododendrons such as the pale *Rhododendron* 'Sir Charles Lemon', and *R. sinogrande*, set off by red *R. thomsonii* make this one of the best spots to be in the early season. Around a dell nicknamed The Boonery (after the Boon family who donated much of its planting) are tender trees and shrubs such as myrtle *Luma apiculata*, the elegant Japanese umbrella pine *Sciadopitys verticillata*, grown for its rich red trunk and glossy leaves, and a most beautiful pine with dense clusters of long delicate needles which is probably the long-needled form of *Pinus rudis*.

From the informal slopes, you turn into the formality of the Fountain Court, with its generous scalloped fountain, backed by impressive flower-filled terraces, with the towers and turrets of the castle crowning the clifftop beyond. These wide terraces, the mildest place in the garden, were famed for their fruit and flowers. They were thought to have been extensively reworked by Adam. An early description, by William Abercummie in 1693, made special mention of 'pretty gardens and orchards, adorned with excellent terases, and the walls loaden with peaches, apricotes, cherries and other fruit'. Half a century later the estate accounts recorded details of espaliers and wall fruit, and in the 19th century John Claudius Loudon reckoned Culzean to be ranked above all other Ayrshire residences for the quality of its parks and gardens.

Today the terrace fruit consists of a huge actinidia by the orangery and the exotic pineapple guava *Acca sellowiana*. They keep company with many other tender shrubs from all over the world: wavy-leaved olearias, bottle brush callistemons, dainty-leafed mimosas and leptospermum among

▲ Embothrium in flower in front of the superb restored glasshouse range

◀◀ View over the Fountain Court and the terraces to the castle

▲ The vinery, with scarlet pelargoniums 'Caroline Schmidt'

▲ Looking down toward the sundial in the walled garden

them. There are trachycarpus and banana plants on the lowest level, in the Fountain Court border, and cordylines that have grown well since they were cut back by the last serious freeze in the winter of 1995/6. This is a border of dramatic plants for bold foliage effect such as cardoon *Cynara cardunculus*, Scotch thistle, *Onopordum*, the tall, pale pink *Dahlia imperialis*, miscanthus grass and summer plantings of canna lilies and abutilons.

The woodland walk to the southeast of the property, is called Happy Valley, probably a homage to Samuel Johnson's *Rasselas*, written in 1759, an influential narrative rejecting the optimisms of Rousseau and Leibnitz, fourteen years before he undertook his Scottish journey with Boswell. The Happy Valley of that book was 'filled with verdure and fertility', with rivulets, birds, animals, music and seclusion, a place where 'every desire was immediately granted'.

In Culzean's valley, a path runs alongside a bright stream that is bricked in one part to create a better flow of water through the watercress beds that were there in the 19th century. At the end of the valley lies the Pagoda and lake known as the Swan Pond. Wonderful trees grow on the slopes of the valley, towering over woodland flowers such as spring daffodils and bluebells, and bright rhododendrons. There is birdsong and sometimes the ravens and peregrines that nest in the cliffs can be seen. It is a place of beauty and refuge, rather than detention as in Johnson's satire.

Continued tree planting coupled with the strong growth of existing trees had made the valley dark and overgrown, so it has been the task of gardeners and estate workers to use the winter months to clear and thin the darkest areas, and already the azaleas, rhododendrons and ground flora are responding. It is also now possible to get a clear view of some of the best trees: some stupendous beeches, firs, wellingtonias and Scots pine, late-flowering eucryphias, parrotia with its rich atumun colour, and the evergreen Chinese fir *Cunninghamia lanceolata*. Robert Adam is thought to have had the responsibility for the development of the early garden. Subsequent work may have been carried out by a person who appears as 'Mr White' in notes in the 12th Earl's *Day Orderly Book*. This may be Thomas White (junior) the proprietor of a successful landscape gardening business. His father, also a well-known designer, had worked as foreman for Capability Brown.

Culzean Castle its policies and 228 hectares of surrounding land came to The National Trust for Scotland from the 5th Marquess of Ailsa in 1945, and in 1969 the policies and gardens were designated Scotland's first country park. An enormous amount of work has been carried out on buildings restoration including the forty architectural elements in the gardens and policies (mostly dating from the time of the 12th Earl) which themselves are now being much more ingeniously managed, to reflect the concerns and interests of the 18th century and a wider picturesque landscape as well as to satisfy the expectations of a 21st-century visitor.

▲ Border with various astilbes and the fan palm, *Trachycarpus fortunei*

Drum Castle

The historic landscape of the Drum Castle, 150 hectares of the once vast estates of the Irvines of Drum, is made up of choice parkland, a walled garden, lawns, an arboretum and the Old Wood of Drum, the last remnant of the oakwoods of lower Deeside. The Old Wood is a favourite place to walk for visitors to the castle and has biological and ecological importance. All four species of British crow are resident, with two substantial rookeries; there are bats and abundant invertebrate life.

Drum has always been significant: castle and wood figure together in the earliest maps. The wood was part of the royal hunting forest at least as early as 1247, and given by Robert the Bruce to William de Irwin in 1323. Timber for St Machar's Cathedral and the Bishop's Palace in Old Aberdeen is believed to have come from Drum and in the early 16th century, it would have formed part of Aberdeen's contribution to James IV's fleet. 'Wode of Drum' timber was used in 1606 to build the *Bon*

◀ The 17th-century rose garden focused on the lion statue and box-edged pool and *Rosa gallica*

71

▲ View from the 20th century garden to the 19th-century garden and *Rosa* 'Frühlingsgold' ▼

Accord, the first large ship to be built and launched at Aberdeen. Drum is part of the cultural fabric of Aberdeen, and still held in high esteem by the people of the city, only ten miles away.

Despite fluctuating fortunes the castle remained in the Irvine family until 1975 when it was bequeathed to The National Trust for Scotland on the death of the 24th laird. The oldest part is the 13th-century tower of pale pink and grey granite, beside which is a Jacobean mansion with Victorian additions. A 17th-century formal garden, described by a contemporary historian as having 'pleasant garden planting' was believed to have been destroyed by Covenanters in 1644. Remains of this and an 18th-century formal garden below the South Lawn were indicated in preliminary soundings by the University of Bradford in 1988. Further exploration is an exciting prospect, possibly of national as well as regional significance.

During the relatively stable times of by Alexander Irvine, the 18th laird (1761–1844), the parkland landscape was developed, and a 1.8-hectare walled garden built in 1796. Earlier kitchen gardens would typically have been snug by the castle, but 18th-century fashion placed them at a distance: at Drum, 200 metres to the northeast. A new south entrance to the castle was made in the 1770s, its drive curving through the park. The late-9th-century extensions switched the main entrance to the north, involving a new eastern drive, conifer-lined with open views northwards, which remains the present approach.

The name Drum derives from the Gaelic for a ridge or knoll: you notice the gentle rise as you enter the estate. There are fine trees all around, many planted in the 19th century, such as Brewer's spruce *Picea breweriana*, Norway maple and wellingtonias. The fine Douglas firs are thought to have been raised from seed collected by Douglas in 1827, and admiration is claimed also by lovely full-grown oaks, limes, sycamores and horse chestnuts. A number of 19th-century paintings of Drum by James Giles, Hugh Irvine, G.E. Forbes and Anna Forbes Irvine show handsome trees on their own or in clumps in the parkland.

A plan of the walled garden from the end of the 18th century shows wide perimeter paths, crossing north-south and east-west axial paths, and an orchard in the north of the garden. The 1865 Ordnance Survey map and an aerial photograph of 1946 indicate little change to the historic plan. A charming photograph of 1884 shows rose arches and pillars with billowing roses and other ornamental plants.

The walled garden was a well-maintained, working produce and flower garden when the Trust took on the property, but was allowed to deteriorate, and it was grassed over in 1988. The new plan for a Garden of Historic Roses dispensed with the old pathways and the produce, but picked up the rose theme of the earlier period. The new layout by Eric Robson, then Head of Gardens, was loosely based on four centuries of rose-growing and design. The 17th- and 18th-century sections were based on illustrations from Sir Frank Crisp's influential book, *Mediaeval Gardens*. This rose garden was completed in 1991, but has been remodelled and adapted to take account of the cold conditions, especially at the lower eastern end. Hardier rose cultivars have been substituted for some that perished, and more hedging introduced. Roses are now mixed with other shrubs, perennials and small trees, which gives a more substantial feel to the garden and affords the roses some shelter.

The 17th-century quadrant contains species roses and Rosa Mundi the famous bicolour *Rosa gallica* Versicolor, in a knot garden design. It is centred on a pool with a handsome stone lion that was brought from Pitmedden in 1989. The source for the 18th-century part, featuring the long-lasting, beautifully scented Portland roses, was a German illustration from 1702, adapted for roses, and additional containers and pedestals. The adjacent section aims for a sense of privacy, with yew enclosures like those in a photograph of a 19th-century rose garden in G.C. Taylor's *The Modern Garden*, while the 20th-century sector centres on a paved sunken area with a sundial. A rose-covered gazebo in the centre of the garden with a lavender edging replicates an original at Tyninghame in East Lothian. Against the east wall is a copy of the bench made by Hugh Lorimer for Kellie.

Entering the rose garden through the attractive wrought gate with its holly motif, you feel an openness unusual for a walled garden, especially one with walls 5-metres high. The garden slopes steeply, dropping 3 metres to the east, but the drop that creates the frost pocket also allows views over the far walls over the countryside to Peterculter.

▶ Sweet peas 'Noel Sutton'

Paradoxically, although it represents past periods of rose-growing, the rose garden has a decided 20th-century character.

Hollies are plentiful at Drum, reflecting the holly leaves prominent in the Irvine coat of arms and crest, and the Trust has introduced many new ones. A recent path to the walled garden (which runs over the foundations of a former one, also aligned on the gate) has been lined with holly 'Golden King'. A row of mature hollies grows to the west of this garden, the gaps recently filled. The nearby Pond Garden, created by the 23rd laird in the 1930s (on the site of an old pond, fed by run-off water from the castle) has also been augmented. It had a good structure of mature conifers, including Western hemlock, *Chamaecyparis pisifera* 'Boulevard', the weeping spruce *Picea breweriana*, junipers, and a multi-stemmed yew. The Trust developed this area adding beds of herbaceous waterside plants, such as rodgersias and ornamental grasses and ferns, and supplementing the aquatic plants. 'Air' a concrete cherub was set on an existing quernstone, and a fairy statue in bronze placed on the small island.

A walk though the Drum grounds, especially at quiet times, is pleasantly accompanied by birdsong. Wagtails, tits and warblers flit constantly through the summer garden. Here as often in the Trust's walled gardens, the visitor's attention to the plants is likely to be distracted by oystercatchers, large pied birds with striking orange-red beaks, courting with loud '*myp myp*' cries on top of the walls. Thomas Shepherd writing nearly two centuries ago, caught the sense of spaciousness of Drum: 'The grounds . . . rise in bold swells, and have a largeness of character which assimilates well with the style of the buildings'.

▲ *Rosa* 'Westerland' and rose hips ▲ *Clematis* 'Hagley Hybrid'

73

early as 1950. Only a few of the long flower-stemmed varieties are available, and they require not only gardening skill, but the use of pesticides to keep them alive, thus bringing an environmental concern into the equation. Gardens are a curious art form; it is in their nature to change. How far is a matter of judgement. There are no right answers, and the approbation of posterity will vary with garden fashion and cultural change.

Each end of the great border transforms itself into a shrub border. To the south, where the tree canopy is denser, there is a fine show of hostas, hardy geraniums and other shade-tolerant plants. Here, too, is a huge draught board, and an armillary sphere commemorating Michael Crichton Stuart and Barbara his wife. There is also a small information centre in the style of a weaver's cottage, designed and made at the same time.

Two large urns, strikingly planted with the ornamental grape *Vitis coignetiae* and gentian *Gentiana sino-ornata*, preside over the northern end of the border. Here also is the tennis court building and a water garden and yew hedge. A superb view back to the palace, takes in the *loaning* with its upswept east range border curving to the upper level of the garden, its height accentuated by Lawson cypresses, part of the Cane planting.

The northern end of the garden holds the Cane water garden with its raised ponds and water lilies, the glasshouse with its superb red 'Mrs Morris' pelargoniums and a walled garden. Fife comes from the Danish, meaning 'wooded country', and although the woodlands of the ancient How of Falkland, with their wild boar and deer have disappeared, there is still open forest to be seen from the palace garden. Part of the story of Walter Scott's later novel *The Fair Maid of Perth* takes place at Falkland Palace which preserves a strong sense of history.

▶ Delphiniums with *Achillea filipendulina*

▼ A historic postcard of the old lupin border

Fyvie Castle

The landscape of Fyvie Castle speaks to you of both its 18th- and 19th-century past and of new beginnings as you sweep round the impressive drive though spacious parkland and set foot in the grounds. The pleasant parking area was once a part of the famous triple-walled garden. The elegant semicircular steps at the southern end led to a raised terrace with some fine statuary. From the marble figure of Paris erected by Alexander Forbes-Leith, it was possible to look down to the wood-edged lake, built by an earlier owner, General Gordon. The lake is still there, the renowned woodland garden known as Rhymer's Haugh has been partly restored, with further development planned over the next few years, but the statue of Paris is thought too fragile to be sited outdoors. In a new development, a modern garden designed as a celebration of Scottish fruits and vegetables has been created in the adjacent area of the great old kitchen garden, marking a reawakening for Fyvie.

◀◀ The walled garden and the main east-west path
◀ The handsome sculptural information board

The sculpture of
Paris, which it was
hoped would go into
the new Scottish fruit
and vegetable garden

The surrounding landscape also changed and developed. The word *fyvie* means 'deer hill' and it is thought the site was originally bleak with sparse trees, the fortified castle occupied a superb defensive situation on a low eminence inside a loop of the River Ythan surrounded by bogland that would impede attack. Geophysical evidence indicates the possible presence of a timber-built castle that may have preceded the stone construction. There was definitely a reference to a Fyvie Castle early in the 13th century, on account of a charter having been granted there in 1222. Roy's Military Survey of 1748-55 shows three fields with trees in them around Fyvie House, as it was known for another two centuries.

It is likely that there were earlier gardens of some kind, but the first known record is of the large kitchen garden in three sections made by General Gordon in 1777. The plan made by John Innes in 1822 showed that the Ball Green contained a fig house (thought to have been one of the earliest in Scotland). The adjacent section Rhymers Haugh grew fabulous mulberries, peaches nectarines, grapes and other fruits. The third part, to the south, was known as 'the Garden used as a Shrubbery'.

In the 19th century, the Ball Green, close to the estate offices, was laid out as a kitchen garden and a vast and beautiful range of glasshouses was built, none of which survives. Fruit and vegetables were grown there until the Second World War but in the second half of the century fortunes flagged. Ball Green was grassed, with limited production of cut flowers and fruit. The National Trust for Scotland saw promise in this area of nearly a hectare that fitted its overall intention to restore some of the most significant features of the designed landscape at Fyvie.

The design for the new garden to celebrate Scottish fruits and vegetables was by Robert Grant

Unlike some castles, which are indissolubly linked with a single great family, the Fyvie estate passed from the possession of the kings of Scotland in 1370 through the families of Preston, Meldrum, Seton, Gordon and Leith. Alexander Seton, Chancellor of Scotland, enlarged and developed Fyvie into one of the finest examples of the Scottish baronial, with its five towers, sculpted dormers, carved finials, crow-stepped gables, skewputs and bartizans. Other families added according to their means and fashion, until the last splendid additions of the Forbes-Leiths in the 19th century. In 1984, Sir Andrew Forbes-Leith sold the castle and its 48-hectare grounds to the Trust.

who is also Regional Gardens Adviser for properties cared for by The National Trust for Scotland in the Northeast region. He was indirectly inspired by the geometries of the plasterwork in the castle entrance hall and of Lord Leith's drawing room in the Gordon Tower. Fruits from Fyvie had been renowned in the past, and the new garden will explore what can be done horticulturally so far north. The new garden, patterned in geometric beds edged with granite setts, is arranged around a central statue of the goddess Gaia, on generous loan from the sculptor, Candida Bond. She presides over a pleasing herb border of rosemary, lavender, sage and thyme.

While the ground was being prepared, plants for the garden were being sourced or propagated. Planting started in 2001 and the garden was beginning to look fuller by 2004. Great square fruit cages (20 metres each side) designed to develop into a solid summertime block of foliage and fruit contain varieties of apple, blackcurrant, raspberries and other berries grown in Scotland. The challenge is far greater for the present Head Gardener, Kevin Wright, than for his predecessors owing to the lack of greenhouse facilities and far fewer staff.

Each fruit cage has a surround of four triangular beds in which Scottish vegetables are cropped in rotation. This gives people a chance to see that plants such as potatoes can be decorative as well as productive. The famous 'Duke of York' which is popular all over Britain was actually raised by William Sim of Fyvie. Some of the uncommon varieties such as 'Edzell Blue' or 'Orkney Black' make a special feature and modern kinds such as 'Brodick' and 'Brodie', bred in the 1990s, also have a place. Other vegetables include cauliflowers 'Balmoral' and 'Castlegrant'; kale 'Pentland Brig'; leek 'Musselburgh', onion 'Ailsa Craig' and swede 'Angus'.

The planned Scottish apple collection will be one of the most complete in Britain, and it is hoped that in the course of its development many varieties that exist only in private collections will be rediscovered and propagated. The apples are grown on different rootstocks, and in different ways: as standard trees, and trained as goblets, cordons, espaliers table-top and step-over. Plums and pears (including the 'Green Pear of Yair' and 'Chalk') are cordoned or espaliered against the south-facing wall. There is also a small nut wood in the easterly section of the garden, beyond a growing collection of rhubarbs.

Gourds add a splash of colour and exoticism, while the south-facing border against the long north wall has bulbs and ornamental plants in it. Some of these are cut to provide flowers for the castle. Glamorous new benches specially designed with an espalier pattern, topped by the Seton crescent, provide places to rest while enjoying the productive scene.

South from the walled garden lies the lake which was designed by Robert Robinson for General William Gordon on the area that was originally peatbog. Improvements were carried out later by James Giles, the artist and landscape designer, who was also a friend of William Gordon in the early 19th century. The lake is fed from the Skeugh Burn and the River Ythan. The parkland surrounding the house was drained and planted with trees at this time. On the 1869 Ordnance Survey map, the landscape had all its principal features, including the boathouse, most of which survive in some form today and a circuit of the lake is still a most enjoyable experience, providing a semi-natural combination of wildness and designed effects.

The westerly garden that was first a shrubbery, then a rose garden, now displays a selection of North American plants to celebrate the historical link between Alexander Forbes-Leith the steel magnate and his wife, with the United States.

⬆ Marigolds and other flowers in the walled garden

▲ A watercolour of Fyvie Castle by James Giles who is said to have had a hand in improving the parkland

83

Geilston

There is something for every taste in the beautifully groomed gardens at Geilston. Around the stone country house with its stables and beautifully proportioned doocoot, is a 4-hectare estate with two large enclosed gardens that contain fruit and vegetables, a prairie, shrub borders, a double herbaceous border and a heather garden and glasshouse. There is a small woodland garden alongside the Geilston Burn, and some fine trees in the sloping lawns. Their well-groomed appearance is a testimonial to the perfectionist principles of the Head Gardener, Joanna Gough, and her assistants. She regards Geilston as 'the ultimate garden for a horticulturist' because 'it has something of everything – ornamentals, fruit, vegetables, water and woodland.'

Geilston House is a mid-18th-century country house, built on the on the outskirts of Cardross looking over the attractive Firth of Clyde, by James Donald, a Glasgow shipping merchant who had

◀◀ The mill pond waterfall and Geilston Burn
◀ Part of the kitchen garden looking westward over young sweetcorn, chard, dill and courgettes

Spring azaleas: the scented *Rhododendron luteum* and various Japanese azaleas and rhododendrons in the walled garden, with small, recently planted golden yews edging the border beyond.

until 1984 when it was replanted with red-twigged lime *Tilia platyphyllos* 'Rubra'. The Geils of Greenock, business partners of James Donald, bought the house in 1805. Miss Lorna Hendry, who gave Geilston to The National Trust for Scotland in 1989, was the daughter of a tenant of Thomas Geils who had bought the house in 1922. She and her friend Miss Bell, and their devoted gardener, had maintained the garden's horticultural excellence and innovation for well over a quarter of a century.

The walled garden that adjoins the house, was built about 1797 – the date on the keystone, and has always been a pleasure garden. A watercolour dated August 1831 shows it planted, as now, with trees and shrubs, the house, lawns and paths just as they are today. The fine wellingtonia in the lower lawn was an early planting and a huge royal fern *Osmunda regalis*, by the top entrance is over 70 years old. There is a superb variety of plants: a bright early summer show of scented azaleas by the house, and shade-loving white trilliums *Trillium grandiflorum* in the west border. There are well-pruned shrubs: spiraeas, fuchsias, hydrangeas, euonymus, and dogwood, and also small flowers such as snowdrops and anemones. A show-stopping double border is densely planted with penstemons, daylilies, hostas, lupins, astilbes, oriental poppies, ligularias and other colourful plants that are grown so well in Scotland.

The attractive heather garden hugs a rocky slope by the house, and the double border runs from here towards the large glasshouse against the lower wall. Built between 1860 and 1899, this fine Mackenzie and Moncur design replaced another on the same spot (marked on the 1860 Ordnance Survey map). There is a most unusual window in the wall inside the small potting shed, near to the glasshouse that gives a view out and over the burn and woodland garden beyond.

The garden is labour intensive. The glasshouse is

prospered, trading tobacco and other goods with Virginia. The earliest settlement on the site might have been 14th-century, and there may be traces of a 17th-century building incorporated into the later building. The Donalds carried out considerable tree planting between 1757 and 1787 and the great lime avenue that lined the main south entrance is believed to have been planted by them. It survived

The Geilston Burn in quiet mood with one of the three bridges that cross it

▲ The kitchen garden, dahlias facing marjoram, blue (and white) *Agastache rugosa* and monarda

▶ The north of the walled garden with its glasshouse and potting shed, with Mrs Ann Hendry, Miss Eliza Hendry and Lorna Hendry as a little girl (who gave Geilston to the Trust). *c.* 1930s

in constant use 'The vegetable garden rules our lives from April to September' acknowledges Joanna. All of the annuals, vegetables and herbaceous plants, including unusual items bought through the internet, are raised from seed, cuttings from the garden or small plant plugs that are brought on in the cold frames. The Trust gardeners, like the previous owners, are interested in trying new plants. One of the latest ideas is the 'meadowesque' prairie garden – the Scots prefer their prairies grass-free – of echinaceas, rudbeckias, heleniums and eupatoriums.

Geilston suffered, like many westerly gardens, from the fungal disease, box blight, and despite efforts to save it, the box around the borders began to look wretched. It was replaced in 2002 with golden yew, the dwarf form of *Taxus baccata* 'Semperaurea' which will be clipped to knee-height. It is now growing well, already making a bright edging.

Geilston has a very large kitchen garden, enclosed by dense beech hedges, situated westwards of the stable block. The 1860 Ordnance Survey and geophysical remains show that paths used to divide it into six sections. At present it is quartered, though the ornamental oval bed at the lower intersection was retained. A large old tank fed by drainage water may have been used for filling watering cans. This garden is being brought back into use in stages. There is a large vegetable section, herbs and soft fruit. It is a formidably productive garden with climbing and runner beans (including the historic bi-coloured variety 'Painted Lady'), onions, spinach, different kinds and colours of courgette, sweet corn, a range of potatoes, peas, cabbages and root vegetables, including carrots, turnips and swedes. Asparagus, herbs and cut flowers are also grown, all of them without chemical sprays, though the garden is not completely organic. A neatly planted young orchard

◀◀ Rhododendrons hybrids sourced by Miss Hendry from Bodnant about 30–40 years ago
◀ Nerines in the sunken garden, the paulownia, with its large leaves, in the rock garden beyond

◀◀ Autumn-red enkianthus, with *Rhododendron yakushimanum*, pale *Pieris japonica* 'Little Heath' and red berberis in the foreground
◀ Rhododendron hybrids, and bluebells

of dessert apples occupies one quarter of the garden, that dips and rises on a south-facing slope. The central double border backed by clipped beech hedges, contains a tumult of dahlias, chrysanthemums and other herbaceous plants and herbs.

Linking the two enclosed gardens, are spacious lawns, dotted with trees and large shrubs, leading down to the burn that twists its way through the wild and naturalised plants and flowering shrubs of the glen. The sound of water tempts the visitor into this delightful woodland area, to a path leading through the glades, and to and fro over the burn.

89

Greenbank Garden

Greenbank Garden in Clarkston, six miles south of Glasgow city centre, stretches away from the symmetry of its 18th-century house in partitions and sections that make it seem much larger than one hectare. The garden is open through the winter, and there is always something to appreciate. For many years the open part of the garden, from the wrought iron gates to the house, was closed to visitors but now the Trust Regional Office is situated in Greenbank House, and the upper garden is also open. It consists of lawn with an avenue of formal yew trees giving a glimpse of the main ornamental garden beyond. There are two curious niches set into the west side of the stone wall quite close to the house which seem a little shallow and too close to the house for bee skeps. The walled garden at Greenbank seems originally to have been designed principally for fruit and vegetables but the area close to the house probably grew ornamental

◀◀ Looking towards the house over the lawn of the upper garden. ◀ *Clematis* 'Comtesse de Bouchaud' with *Echium vulgare* seedlings

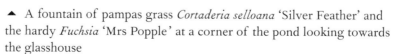

▲ A fountain of pampas grass *Cortaderia selloana* 'Silver Feather' and the hardy *Fuchsia* 'Mrs Popple' at a corner of the pond looking towards the glasshouse

◤ Double flowered *Clematis* 'Purpurea Plena Elegans', *Tropaeolum peregrinum* and *Echium vulgare* seedlings intertwine riotously on a bank

▶ The formal garden in the upper section, infilled with alyssum and heuchera

plants. A small fruit store some distance away was built into the cool east wall of the garden but the function of the two niches remains unresolved.

Greenbank is one of those gardens where time seems to have taken a hop and a skip, so the style of the original house and the garden shape as described in 1771 is almost completely preserved. It was built by Robert Allason, a local merchant, as a celebration of the prosperity that came to him as a result of the expansion of trade and construction in and around the outskirts of Glasgow in the late 18th century. The classic Georgian country house with a walled garden stretching to the south was enclosed by a shelterbelt of woodland. Robert Allason's planned tree-lined avenue to the house from the north got only as far as a small plantation because of a land dispute with a relative, so he made the east-west drive we use as the approach today.

Robert Allason died in 1785, having sold Greenbank, partly as a result of the effects on trade of the American War of Independence. Later owners also found that their fortunes fluctuated and the ownership of Greenbank went through several families until another local man, John Hamilton, who came from East Kilbride, became the first of four generations of Hamiltons to own it; but they made little change apart from adding a new south porch. Over the years, Clarkston developed from a country village into a prosperous suburb but Greenbank was protected from encroachment by its surrounding land.

In 1962, W.P. Blyth, from nearby Busby, bought Greenbank, and he and his wife began work on the ornamental garden. Fifteen years later, he gave the property to The National Trust for Scotland, with the desire that it should serve as a garden advice centre for the owners of suburban gardeners. Jim May, who has been Head Gardener since then, has faithfully pursued this objective. Greenbank con-

tains about 4000 named cultivars and is a centre for plant trials; it holds the National Collection of bergenias, and a large narcissus collection. It is divided into many small enclosed areas designed to offer ideas and practical schemes to gardeners.

The soil at Greenbank is heavy clay, so impervious that a quantity of it was transported to Culzean Castle for the repuddling of their ponds. It must be said that such ground is not idea for gardening but the walled garden at Greenbank has been cultivated for centuries. With humus and lime added, such heavy, acid clays become more easily workable, though plants still suffer from late and lingering frosts and waterlogged soils. This garden shows that much can be grown in conditions that are as challenging as any to be found in Scotland.

There are over thirty different enclosures leading one into another, separated by dense borders, and hedges of yew or privet. Even the old bull pen has been put to use, converted into a paved garden and the small Diamond Jubilee parterre. The pattern of the Jubilee parterre, picked out in box, is the fleur de lys of the Duke of Rothesay (The Prince of Wales) who is patron of The National Trust for Scotland.

Trials of plants for the Consumers' Association (*Gardening from Which*) take place over several years, in beds set aside for the purpose. Recent subjects have included lychnis, hemerocallis, mallows, delphiniums and nepeta. Many perennials are put through their paces here. Once the trial reports have been made, the plants are used elsewhere in the garden. Occasionally they have been sent to other Trust gardens. In 1999 for example, fifteen varieties of delphinium went to Haddo House.

Colour contrast is the theme of the adjacent borders, where hot bright reds and oranges can be compared with soft cool blues, creams and whites. One of these wide borders which contains flowering

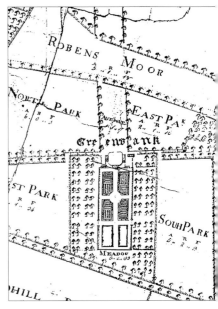

▲ A 1772 plan of Greenbank

▲ An aerial shot taken in 1994

◀ Willow *Salix lanata* bursting into leaf

shrubs such as *Viburnum rhytidophyllum* and *Amelanchier canadensis* is thought may contain some of the Blyths' old planting. This area of the garden is soon to be redeveloped as a border of plants with foliage of special interest.

At the centre of the garden, beds backed by crisp privet hedges, focus on the sundial. Clipped box mounds that give colour and shape for the winter, are engulfed with annuals in the summer months, with a different theme each year. The ancient sundial of 1620 was restored and the gnomens reinstated in 1997. After some discussion it was agreed that it should be set to Glasgow time, as it would have been when the house was built (Greenwich mean time was not initiated until 1884). Unfortunately the sundial has been subjected to vandalism but there are hopes it can be safely put back into place in the future.

In the area once occupied by the Blyths' tennis court, there is now a glasshouse, pond and several raised beds and stone basins and troughs. Originally, laid out to provide inspiration for less able gardeners, it has become a favourite place in the garden. Exotic and tender plants wintered under glass are plunged into gravel beds here for early colour and to give them an opportunity to grow outdoors for at least part of the year. Raised beds in the sun provide a home for alpine and small plants, and, in a shady corner, ferns thrive.

Bergenias – at the time of writing just over 100 species and named cultivars – are used around the garden but there is also a special bergenia enclosure, set out in the winter of 2003/4, where the plants can be inspected and compared in leaf and in bloom

◀ *Dahlia* 'Sister Clementine' and *Abutilon* 'Savitzii' and *Abutilon pictum* 'Thompsonii' mingling beautifully throughout the year. Bergenias and other foliage plants also border the quiet, hedged garden containing the leaping water nymph fountain by Pilkington Jackson in a round pool. Greenbank also has good number of phlox, some of these beautifully scented old plants possibly historic Clyde Valley varieties. These may form part of a National Plant Collection, which, it is hoped, will later be grown here.

In the garden to the west, spring brings many of the 350 named daffodils into flower. The Greenbank daffodil day on which as many as possible of the cultivars are exhibited, is now an annual event, organised by the local Friends of Greenbank who have done much over the years to sustain and support the garden. In the 1920s, Major Hamilton (a narcisissarian) bought many special bulbs. Some came from Brodie Castle in Moray where a National Plant Collection of Brodie daffodils is now maintained. Old nursery invoices at Greenbank show that Hamilton was prepared to pay high prices for his daffodil varieties – as much as £25 for 8-10 bulbs. Some of these have been lost at Brodie, and about forty varieties from Greenbank are going to be grown under controlled conditions for identification. Outside the walled garden, the woodland dell to the northwest brims with snowdrop and daffodils, probably there are yet more named varieties here. Although they have not been studied and identified, they are greatly enjoyed by spring visitors.

A very old apple tree just to the west of the glasshouse is a relic from the days when the garden was given over to orchard and kitchen garden. It is culinary and still fruits, but also provides a support for a white climbing rose. It was thought to be a kind of *Rosa* x *centifolia* when it was planted but it grows with such vigour that Jim May has doubts about this identification. It produces a mass of white flowers in early summer and scarlet hips in autumn.

Greenbank is continually developing and changing. Features showing how new plant associations and horticultural ideas can be implemented in Scottish conditions include a border of grasses, an area with cottage garden plants and gardens that demand less bending and ground work. A demonstration bed of direct sown annuals shows how well they can bloom in Scotland. Herbs also have a place, and large and small-scale topiary in yew and box. Clematis are also a speciality of this garden, especially those that bloom in early summer. Greenbank is loved and loyally supported by the local population, and people returning regularly make up a large proportion of visitor numbers.

▲ Looking over the pool in the lower garden with waterlilies and selection of aquatic and marginal plants

Haddo House

The great house at Haddo is swathed in its vast billowing lawns, some of them banking off the paths at an alarming angle for the gardeners to mow. Former buildings on the site such as the fortified keep of Kellie, which was ransacked by Covenanters in 1644, had used the site defensively, but William Gordon, the 2nd Earl of Aberdeen, had set his sights on a new building, quite different in character. He commissioned the architect William Adam to build a large, elegant, Palladian mansion.

The new mansion named Haddo House was built of finely worked ashlar, cut on site from rubble stone possibly from Pitmedden, and the best imported roof timbers and finest lime. The notable Aberdeen builder John Baxter wrote in the autumn of 1732 of good progress being made although they were using 'white asheller all wrought wt. Hamers which is a longesom work'. The entrance from the west had an elegant double stairway, while an

◄◄ Looking through the huge rose, probably *Rosa mulliganii* by the clock tower of the South Range
◄ View from the lower beds of hardy geranium and campanula to the northwest of the house

97

▲ James Giles
watercolour of the
terrace at Haddo

expansive grass terrace to the east dropped to a long avenue double lined with lime trees, leading the eye to the distant hillside. Pavilions to the north and south were linked to the main building by curved corridors. William Gordon had stepped outside the stylistic architectural conventions of the time, but though he was said to be 'very absolout in his own opinion' he had the advice of the able Sir John Clerk of Penicuik and through him the services of William Adam and John Baxter.

This impressive new house is thought to have looked out on to open country. The great avenue led across a peat moss through which ran the Kellie Burn. At the beginning of the 19th century, the 4th Earl of Aberdeen (Prime Minster from 1852–1855) took an interest in improvements at Haddo. It had been neglected, and he confided in a letter dated October 1833 that though he had arrived safely, 'The gloom and desolation of the place can scarcely be endured'. Undeterred, he began a series of changes and developments that made the house grander and more massive, and changed the surrounding landscape.

He was a formidable tree-planter. He called on the services of James Giles, the artist and landscape designer to advise him on the making of a chain of three lakes, which would drain the moss. Thousands of trees could then be planted in what could now be described as a landscape park. The 4th Earl erected a huge urn, possibly to his first wife, Catherine, at the end of the avenue. It was inscribed, with ironic Scots understatement, *Haud immemor* (Not unmindful). He raised an obelisk to the southwest of the house, in memory of his brother Alexander Gordon who had fallen at Waterloo.

The 4th Earl elaborated the raised east terrace, with paths and geometrical flowerbeds edged with kerbing tiles. These beds were designed to taper in the view from the house, in order to give the

impression that the vast terrace was even larger than it was. Each tile fits precisely with its neighbour, so they may only be laid in a particular order. The central fountain was in place by 1836, which was the year water began to be let into the lake. Looking out over the terrace two years later, the Earl could write with satisfaction that 'the view of the lake from the Drawing Room windows is now made very good indeed.' By 1848 all the flowerbeds were finished.

Since then, the view to the lake has been obscured by some fine trees, including wellingtonias planted by Queen Victoria and Prince Albert, about 1857. The effect has been to frame the terrace and to give it greater emphasis. James Giles' paintings of it ensure that the Trust has a clear idea of the original layout and the character of the planting in the mid-19th century.

During the Second World War, potatoes were grown on the terrace as part of the 'Dig for Victory' campaign (while the house was used as a maternity hospital). In 1946, June Aberdeen and her father-in-law, the 3rd Marquess of Aberdeen and Temair, laid it out to roses. In 2002, the roses, which had become sick, were removed and the soil cleaned and planted with bedding for two years to rest the soil, exhausted by sixty years of rose growing. Keith Blundell, the Head Gardener has explored a number of different planting themes in his tenure at Haddo. Modern bedding plants such as petunias are used, but he has tried to find a few from a palette of bedding plants and perennials that were popular in late Regency and Early Victorian times. The choice is surprisingly large and various. Early varieties of pelargonium, and other plants such as *Phlox drummondii*, ageratum, heliotrope and verbena, were beginning to be popular for bedding

The border known as Cannon Border close to the

house typically has 'Bishop of Llandaff' dahlias contrasting with the pale stone. The lower beds to either side of the terrace contain some plants that have been researched and returned to the garden such as the thalictrum, 'Hewitt's Double' and a double Scotch rose. A delphinium known as 'Haddo' (sold at one time by Bakers Nursery), and the pink 'Dalmarnock' daffodils that once bloomed along the east avenue are feared lost.

James Giles was commissioned to make other paintings of Haddo and of neighbouring castles, since the 4th Earl had intended to publish a book on the castles of Aberdeenshire, but this project was pre-empted by the publication in 1849, of *The Castellated Architecture of Aberdeenshire* by Sir Andrew Leith-Hay of Leith Hall. Giles' watercolours, charming in themselves, are also most informative about garden and landscape. They include depictions of Fyvie Castle, Craigievar, Castle Fraser and the Castle of Gight where Catherine Gordon and Captain Jack Byron (Lord Byron's father) had lived.

In 1877, the 7th Earl married and brought Ishbel Marjoribanks, his wife, to Haddo; at first she thought it a 'horrible house', but they made it comfortable, and Ishbel's interest in photography has left us an invaluable record of the changing schemes of the gardens over a long period. This, in conjunction with estate records, will form the basis of a study on which a future reconstruction of the gardens at Haddo will be based. Gordons still live at Haddo and take an interest in its running, although the house and immediate garden, have been managed by The National Trust for Scotland since 1978 and the 72 hectares of parkland is managed by Aberdeenshire Council as Haddo Country Park.

A small gate marks the end of the garden proper, and leads into the beginning of the avenue, where

wild flowers such as cuckoo flower and blossom from the cherries mingle pleasantly under the purple beech. The beautiful, wrought Golden Gates let you into the parkland beyond, now the Country Park. The mowing height of the grass is agreed between the Trust and the Country Park so as to take the eye into the distant landscape as was originally intended, and the fencing is discreet to create a seamless transition, without any interruption of the view.

▲ From the stately raised terrace, the vista down through the Golden Gates to the park and the stone urn

99

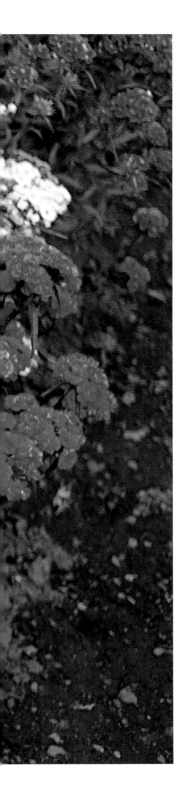

Harmony Garden

Walk down past Melrose Abbey and into the drive of Harmony House and you find yourself in a country town garden that still has a sense of its early 19th-century origins, but has charm for the present day. The house with its views to the Eildon Hills, was built in the Georgian style in 1807 for Robert Waugh, a local man who had started out as a joiner and made a fortune growing allspice (pimento) on the Harmony Estate in Jamaica. The garden, which looks to the ruined abbey on its eastern side, was designed to have a separateness from the bustle of the town, its isolation reflecting the dour character of its owner who was known, even to friends, as Melancholy Jacques. Later the atmosphere cheered and the house passed through five generations of the Curle family. Harmony House, its 1-hectare garden, the gardener's cottage and the grounds opposite, was left in 1996 to The National Trust for Scotland by Mrs Christian Pitman, daughter of the

◀◀ Sweet William and phlox
◀ A view to the distant house from the bluebells of the meadow

▲ The ornamental garden, with the kitchen garden and its wall fruit beyond, and Melrose Abbey

villa (now a listed building). A stupendous double border, four metres each side of a path, used to lead from the flight of stone steps at the main entrance (said to replicate those of the Jamaican Harmony), to the tree-lined south end of the garden, where it linked with the inner perimeter path around the lawn. It was the main drama of the garden in the 1930s, but was grassed over during postwar economies. In the summer of 2004, some beautiful glass plates were rediscovered picturing borders thought to be Harmony or Priorwood.

To the west is a woodland area with hazels, and floods of bluebells under the trees in early summer. Christian Pitman planted its grassy margin with daffodils (including some cultivars, now rare) wild flowers, martagon lilies, fritillaries, and spring and autumn crocuses. She also planted the walnut, just reaching maturity, and two superb wall-trained apricots, both over thirty years old, that produce quantities of sweet fruit. A sunken lawned area, banked on each side, on the west side of the house, may be an old curling pond (Christian Pitman's grandfather was President of the Melrose Curling Association). The borders to the east, backed by a low wall, brim with interesting herbaceous plants and shrubs. There are some striking associations, the dark foliage of Ligularia 'Desdemona' dark against the light green of a large deutzia, or alongside flame-red tiger lilies. The bold purple of mallow 'Braveheart' contrasts with the dark flowers and pleated leaves of the tall *Veratrum nigrum*. There are clematis and honeysuckle by the gateway, and robust hostas, the yellow tree paeony and brilliant dahlias. Bees range the flowers, smothering the round flowerheads, of the tall thistle *Echinops ritro* all summer long.

Flanking the flagged path leading through to the kitchen garden are beautifully planted informal

antiquarian Sir James Curle, with the wish that it should be preserved for the people of Melrose and visitors.

The entrance drive sweeps past a wide border and large rhododendron bed to bring you into the quiet heart of the garden surrounding the house. Open lawns, beautifully tended borders and box-edged beds surround the imposing 19th-century

beds of carefully selected cultivars: double marguerite daisies, *Crocosmia* 'Lucifer' the silvery-leaved *Anaphalis triplinervis*, *Eryngium alpinum* 'Blue Star', rudbeckias, the dwarf willow *Salix lanata* and home-raised white hellebores.

The vegetables and salad produce grown in the kitchen garden remain in keeping with those formerly grown for the family. They include the staples, potatoes, runner beans, beet and the Florence fennel that was a special favourite — though not scorzonera, which wasn't. The long roots of this vegetable break too easily in the clay soil making them difficult to harvest entire. There are apple trees trained against the wall, and a full range of soft fruit including a large bed of the red and white form of the alpine strawberry 'Baron Solemacher'. These delicious small strawberries were also much liked by Christian Pitman. Flower such as sweet peas, and penstemons are also grown in the kitchen garden, and phlox has a special place, the stock here being the remnant from the well-known nursery of Forbes of Hawick.

This nursery had 350 named phloxes in their 1901 catalogue. The cultivar *Phlox paniculata* 'Dodo Hanbury-Forbes' has an Award of Garden merit from the RHS. Some of the flowers from this garden are taken by dried flower experts from nearby Priorwood garden. There is an agreement between the pickers and the Head Gardener, Norman Tait, that no more than a quarter of the blooms be taken, so as not to denude the garden. The vegetables are sold locally as they have been for many years, since the days when Christian Pitman used to invite neighbours and townspeople to pick the fruit in this garden and in the apple orchard across the road from the garden.

Two glass plates from the Curle archive. Mr Jackson with the phlox in the garden in September 1948 and a view of a border in August 1951. These were originally thought to be Harmony, but were very recently reassessed as Priorwood.

The Hermitage

Probably the Trust's most romantic and picturesque property, the Hermitage is a place heavy with Scottish history and symbolic resonance in a setting of extraordinary natural beauty. The 13 hectares of woodland near Dunkeld in Perthshire encircle the wooded gorge of the River Braan and its picturesque folly, known as Ossian's Hall or the Hermitage.

The way to the Hermitage was once cultivated with paths through rock formations, and beds of shrubs and cultivated flowers. Thomas Pennant in *A Tour of Scotland* noted 'a mixture of cultivation with vast rocks springing out of the ground, among which are conducted a variety of walks, bordered with flowers and flowering shrubs and adorned with numbers of little buildings, in the style of Oriental gardens.' The natural beauties of the place were further enriched by supplementary waterways, probably in the form of rills, fed from holding pools higher up, which splashed through rocky streambeds and through moss-covered boulders.

◀ The woodland path that runs alongside the Braan, and the Hermitage perched above the crashing water

▶ The River Braan in quiet mood: an old photograph of the Hermitage and the Hermitage Bridge

Now, more trees have grown and where there were beds and rockeries, are only rough tumbles of rocks and native plants. It is as natural as any of the Romantic heros could have wanted, and picturesque in the touching way of overgrown gardens.

The Hermitage is best visited after a strong fall of rain, when the little River Braan runs high. The path runs along the bank for about a mile. This is a lovely walk to take in late spring when the fresh beech foliage contrasts with the superb conifers along the route. Eventually you see a small oval-shaped building on a rise in the woodland, and making your way upwards, you become aware of the increasing turbulence of the water.

The first chamber of the Hermitage itself is small and quite dark, and you can glimpse the tumult of the falls beyond. Pause for a moment, then step into the larger chamber with its semi-circular open balcony. The noise of the falls is concentrated at the threshold and as you pass in the assault of noise and light is stupendous. The crashing of the falls creates a mist of spray that sends small rainbows all over the balcony. Through the mist you see the rapid rush of white water as the river drops through a narrow ravine over large rocks. It is as impressive

now as when it thrilled Dorothy Wordsworth in 1803. At that time the doorway between the two chambers was concealed by a panel, on which was painted a portrait of the legendary Scots poet Ossian, that would be slid back suddenly by a guide to allow entrance to the 'splendid room, which was almost dizzy and alive with waterfalls, that tumbled in all directions – the great cascade, which was opposite to the window that faced us, being reflected in innumerable mirrors upon the ceiling and against the walls.'

The Wordsworths 'laughed heartily at the contrivance', though William later disparaged the 'Intrusive Pile, ill-graced with baubles of theatric taste'. The Reverend William Gilpin, who had sterner definitions of the picturesque, thought it over-adorned and that ' the native forest wood, the natural brush of the place had been sufficient. Instead of this, the path, which winds among fragments of rock, is decorated with knots of shrubs and flowers. . . . Such ideas in scenes dedicated to grandeur and solitude, are incongruous.' He was however, impressed by 'one of the grandest, most beautiful cascades we have ever seen.'

The present walk to the falls has perhaps the best of both worlds: the fine trees and river, wild flowers and history and the additional romance of an overgrown garden within a wild setting. There are no baubles, or red and blue stained glass, or Claude Lorraine glasses; the inside of the Hermitage is bare although the plasterwork gives a sense of past ornament. Since it was built in 1757, the building has several times fallen into ruin and been repaired. It was vandalised in 1821, and in 1869 it was blown up. In 1944 the Hermitage lands passed to The National Trust for Scotland. The Trust's 1951 restoration was by Basil Spence in the early days of his architectural career. Further work on the floor and walls was done in the 1980s.

The Hermitage has the distinction of having been a landscape tourist attraction for well over two hundred years. It began with an idea of the young John Murray (later to be the 3rd Duke of Atholl) who in 1757 constructed a small summerhouse at the Black Linn Falls for his uncle, the 2nd Duke.

Around the Hermitage was a walled garden of about a quarter of an acre and apple trees, figs, quince and strawberries. Later, with the building of the Hermitage Bridge, a graceful arched footbridge across the Braan, in 1774, the surrounding landscape began to be developed into a substantial woodland garden with the planting of trees and ornamental plants, and the construction of walls and walks. A little higher up the river, are two structures named by the Trust: Ossian's Cave and Ossian's Seat. The 'cave' (mentioned by Gilpin in 1776), made on the basis of a natural rock formation, is of rough unadorned rock, with a roof and small windows. Nearby is a low stone bench known as Ossian's Seat.

In 1782-3, the summerhouse was remodelled by the 4th Duke's architect George Steuart, decorated with elaborate gilt plasterwork, mirrors and coloured glass and renamed Ossian's Hall. The garden historian Christopher Dingwall who has pieced together much of the early history of the Hermitage has discovered a good deal of circumstantial evidence to suggest that the emphasis on Ossian was a symbolic means of paying homage to the Jacobite traditions and royalist kinsmen of the Dukes of Atholl. Interest in Ossian was greatly increased by James Macpherson's influential and popular translations and elaborations of Ossianic literature in epics such as *Fingal* and *Temora*. The Jacobite struggle and Scottish heritage in general were assuming a new cultural significance.

Throughout the late 18th century the planting of

▲ A view of the falls from the balcony of the Hermitage

trees and other plants continued at The Hermitage, so that the landscape which had been fairly open rocky moorland in 1750 became progressively more wooded. Accounts of the years 1787-92 credited the Duke of Atholl with having planted more than 3 million trees. A new element was added in 1861 with the railway route from Dunkeld that passed through the Hermitage grounds by way of an elegant viaduct.

The Hermitage has attracted dukes, earls and many crowned heads of Europe, poets, painters and composers. Robert Burns, the Wordsworths, Turner, Mendelssohn and Queen Victoria all visited. It was reckoned that the grounds of Dunkeld and the Hermitage had received 60,000 visitors between 1814 and 1842. They came first by horse, then train and now that the new A9 delivers you direct to the path to Ossian's Hall, more visitors than ever arrive by car. Military aircraft fly overhead and you bikers skim along the footpaths, but nonetheless, this beautiful landscape retains its solitary beauty and capacity to enchant.

The Hill House

There is still a magical view from Upper Helensburgh over the town below and down to the Clyde, although there are many more buildings than there were when the Glasgow publisher Walter Blackie chose this place for his family house. He was advised to entrust the young Charles Rennie Mackintosh (with whom his sister-in-law was acquainted through art college) with its design. Walter was aware of the history of Scottish architecture: the fortified tower, the mansions, the Scottish baronial. He knew the style of Alexander Thomson (who designed Holmwood and also worked for the firm of Blackie). He had specific ideas about his new family house. He liked slate roofing, preferred harling to brick, and, as a matter of principle, wished for architectural effect 'to be secured by the massing of the parts rather than by adventitious ornament'.

As it turned out Charles Rennie Mackintosh introduced most of the ornamentation he desired, but

◀◀ Looking up to the house from the rock garden
◀ The house with the pepperpot gardener's hut

only after he had convinced his patron of its necessity. There seems to have been a happy collaboration between a patron of discrimination and an architect with impressive talent, thoroughness and attention to practical and aesthetic detail. The Hill House with its clean verticals and bold outline, its L-shape, grey harling, and mock towers, connects with Scottish building of the past, at the same time representing an unequivocal expression of its own period.

A building as elegant as The Hill House requires a distinctive setting. Mackintosh is known to have suggested the semicircular lawn at the entrance drive, and terrace walls, perfect for climbing plants. Horseshoe shaped openings in these walls allow views of the house from the garden. The small gardener's hut is in the shape of a pepperpot tower (similar to those at Castle Fraser). Walter Blackie was a knowledgeable gardener, and it is likely that his input to the layout was considerable. A picture from 1915 shows him inspecting a standard rose in the rose garden with every evidence of enjoyment. The overall design of the main garden divisions is similar to an early plan by Mackintosh, but the upper lawn was

◀ Walter Blackie in the Rose garden

▶ The mound with its bluebells and young birches

left clear below a long border by the Blackies, rather than being subdivided into nine square subsections.

The hillside site allows for an easy relationship between house, garden and wider landscape. From almost everywhere in the garden the silver-grey bulk of the house provides a reference point, and allows for an appreciation of the different faces and surfaces of the building. There are fine trees, but the house was – and remains, uncluttered. It gives a subliminal impression of an ocean liner, sailing on its green lawns, echoing the ships far below on the Clyde, seen from the upper windows. From the bay window of the gloriously bright drawing room the different areas of the garden beckon giving a sense of light and spaciousness.

The garden was overgrown when the property came to The National Trust for Scotland in 1982. The restoration of the house took priority, and was beautifully carried out. Attention was then given to renovating the garden, especially to recreating the clean lines of its original composition. They were guided by the recollections of Mrs Blackie and Miss

Agnes Blackie, Walter's daughter-in-law and daughter, and pictures from an article published in 1905 in *Deutsch Kunst und Dekoration*.

The first view of the garden is the semi-formal entrance drive. Stately blue mop-head hydrangeas line the wall, and a half-circle of small clipped standard hollies follow the curve of the lawn. The hollies are a Scottish cultivar of common holly, *Ilex aquifolium* 'Scotica' which has dark dense foliage without prickles, and takes well to the lollipop clipping. During Walter Blackie's time the kitchen garden was uphill to the north of the house, but the Trust has sited the kitchen garden (mainly of vegetable varieties used in the Edwardian era) around the glasshouse that survives from a range built by Walter Blackie in the northeast corner. There is a neatly mown apple orchard in the grassed area to the north, and, immediately beside the house, a kinetic sculpture given to the garden by George Rickey. This space had originally been reserved for a distinctive feature, but a wellhead, suggested by Mackintosh, had been vetoed on the grounds of cost.

The sunny southern courtyard has ornamental quinces *Chaenomeles* x *superba* 'Knap Hill Scarlet' and the white *C. speciosa* 'Nivalis', the tall, sky-blue *Ceanothus arboreus* 'Autumnal Blue' and several bourbon roses and other flowering climbers and wall-trained shrubs. The top walk is entered through an arch of *clematis* 'Ville de Lyon' and 'Comtesse de Bouchaud' and the scented, early 20th-century roses 'Bleu Magenta' and 'Gerbe Rose'.

A small orchard along the east side, established by the Blackies in a wild-flower meadow, has been restored. Native and naturalised plants grow together here: spring daffodils, snake's-head fritillaries, cowslips, camassias, red campion, dog daisy, summer foxgloves, bellflowers, orange hawkweed and hemp agrimony. Nearby the 'lilac circle', thought to have been a Mackintosh suggestion, and a neat rose garden have been reinstated. Throughout the garden, plants that were available in the early decades of the last century have been given preference. This principle will apply in the rose garden, which is in the process of transformation. Its once-trim box hedging succumbed to box blight, and is being replaced with box-leaved holly *Ilex crenata*.

Roses are a special theme of the dining room at the Hill House. Margaret Macdonald Mackintosh – who according to her husband was 'the genius' – contributed to the decorative design of the Hill House. Her accomplished gesso panel of the sleeping beauty in a thicket of briar roses is the centrepiece of the dining room. Walter's wife, Anna Blackie, admired it greatly, and rose decoration was taken up in wall stencils, and wall lights decorated with stained glass roses.

A double herbaceous border extends to the east of the house, between the orchard and the pepper-pot tower. An attractive country house border rather than an elegant setpiece, it contains Edwardian favourites such as the blue, round-headed thistle *Echinops ritro*, lambs' ears *Stachys byzantina*, sweet rocket, hardy geraniums, blue and white forms of Jacob's ladder *Polemonium caeruleum* and perennial honesty *Lunaria rediviva*, which are augmented by unusual herbaceous perennials such as pink-flowered turtlehead *Chelone obliqua* from North America, the Japanese *Kirengeshoma palmata* with its handsome foliage and dark, wiry stems and pale yellow flowers, and the blue wild indigo *Baptisia australis*. The tall leaves of *Iris sibirica* contrast with the frothy flowers of astilbes of different kinds, foliage plants such as *Tellima grandiflora* and heucheras, and the turrets of *Verbascum phoeniceum* and viper's bugloss. Thistles, cosmos and dahlias keep the borders colourful through late summer. In the ample upper lawn, a curious grassy mound is crowned by three graceful young birches *Betula pendula* 'Laciniata' towards the eastern side.

The lower lawn has been levelled – necessarily, since it was originally the site of a croquet lawn and tennis court. Separating the upper and lower lawns is a dense lime hedge with an archway through it, contrasting with the informality of the flowering trees such as *Eucryphia glutinosa* and shrubs along the long western side of the garden.

Several secluded, compartmentalised gardens lie off the sloping western path, where you can find a lily pond, a fern garden, some graceful Japanese maples and a small rock garden of the 'plum pudding' kind, much liked a century ago, but out of fashion nowadays. In and among the rocks are storksbills and cotulas growing with ferns such as hart's-tongue, Japanese shield fern and lady fern. There are many lichens on the rocks throughout this garden, signifying fresh air, although Helensburgh is only 22 miles from Glasgow centre.

Hill of Tarvit Mansionhouse

The mansion and garden of Hill of Tarvit above Cupar in Fife dominate the hillside, inviting the visitor to the fine Edwardian house built by Sir Robert Lorimer for the Dundee financier and jute merchant, Frederick Sharp. Lorimer also designed the fine garden skirting the house. The wide and sloping terraces with their lawns, great trees and generous borders, add considerably to the dignified presence of the property. There is a dynamic interplay between the house and the wider landscape. From the parkland, the eye is drawn back to the mansion; from the mansion and the gardens you are aware always of the surrounding countryside.

Sharp was one of those Scots who participated in and promoted the industrial boom in Scotland in the decades around the turn of the 20th century. He used his fortune to acquire antique furniture and paintings, commissioning the new house specifically to reflect the style and quality of his collections. Hill of Tarvit was also a place for Frederick,

◀◀ *Eryngium alpinum* and ◀ the steps to the middle terrace; the north wall and the woods beyond

113

▲ *Rosa* 'Gloire de Dijon' above a door in the east wall of the garden
◀ *Euphorbia palustris* and *Allium caeruleum*

Beatrice his wife, and their two children to live in and to entertain. It was however a shortlived dynasty as the magnate died in 1932, and his wife in 1946, having been predeceased by their only son. Their daughter Elizabeth lived only a little longer, leaving the house, 4.5-hectare gardens, and additional farmland in the care of The National Trust for Scotland in 1949.

The house Frederick Sharp demolished on his purchase of the property in 1904 had been called Wemyss Hall. Attributed to Sir William Bruce, it had gardens and a landscape park, thought to have been redesigned in late 17th and early 18th centuries. It was in the context of this older landscape that Robert Lorimer designed the formal gardens around the house in 1907. The garden today has a period feel, respecting the formal design. The original rose garden, the setpiece bedding by the entrance and the raised circular beds retain a decided Edwardian character.

In the borders and informal areas the planting has a strong spirit of enterprise with a brilliant mixture of old fashioned and new plants of extraordinary variety and quality. The formality sets off an abundance of plants that spill over the neat paths and terrace walls in carefully monitored abandon.

The sheltered and south-facing top border contains well-grown shrubs and perennials, dotted through with some unusual trees such as the paper mulberry *Broussonetia papyrifera*, and catalpa. There is a beautiful mature hoheria *Hoheria sexstylosa*, generally expected to be tender but thriving this far north (about 20 miles south of Dundee) and 500 feet above

◀ In front of a magnificent *Eucryphia* x *nymanensis* 'Nymansay'; *Eupatorium*, *pupureum* 'Atropurpureum'; *Phlox paniculata* 'White Admiral', *Helenium* 'Moerheim Beauty', and *Rudbeckia* 'Goldquelle'

sea level. Peter Christopher, the Head Gardener here for many years, prefers to alter the line of the path rather than prune this splendid specimen.

Here you find shrubby Edwardian introductions such as leycesteria, lilacs, the elegant mock orange, *Philadelphus* 'Beauclerk' together with big handsome perennials such as the big, pale clary *Salvia sclarea* var. *sclarea*, *Campanula lactiflora*, deep pink sanguisorba and blush-pale, slender-stemmed *Veronicastum virginicum*.

There is masterly orchestration in this border: Japanese anemones in profusion tone beautifully with the colour of the sandstone; a common plant

▲ The interesting shapes of Robert Lorimer's skyline, viewed from the rose garden

Hill of Tarvit
Mansionhouse, elegant
but friendly, *Rosa*
'Rambling Rector' on
the double staircase

▸▸ Hew Lorimer's
basket of fruit in stone

such as the silvery pink *Geranium* x *oxoniarum* looks glamorous next to an unusual species *Geranium asphodeloides* growing liberally around a large purple smoke bush *Cotinus coggygria* 'Royal Purple'. Golds and yellows are the theme of another dramatic grouping of alstroemerias and the small yellow daisies of *Anthemis tinctoria* backed by a tall branching species of elecampane *Inula racemosa*.

Hill of Tarvit is exciting for the gardener both for its plant associations and for the distinction of its plants. Hardy geraniums of many kinds play their part in the borders, including some less usual examples of particular quality such as the blue *G. renardii* cross 'Philippe Vapelle' with its wide-open blue, slightly creased flowers held over a neat low tump of silvery-grey foliage. There are a number of

unusual buddlejas including *Buddleja colvilei* with unusually large flowers almost foxglove-like in magenta bunches. Another is a *Buddleja* x *weyeriana* (a cross between *Buddleja globosa* and *B. davidii*), a late-flowering cultivar with a strong honey scent, which extends the season for insects.

The soil is rich and fertile with a favourably neutral pH. The Hill of Tarvit is a high garden at 500 feet above sea level, but the woodland behind the garden gives shelter and plants thrive there, many of them self-seeding. Outside the walled terraced garden are wilder areas around the lanes. Gardened with a lighter touch, these are full of an exuberant mixture of wild and garden plants. In one shady area large clumps of lilies such as cardiocrinums *Cardiocrinum giganteum*, and tiger lilies *Lilium*

lancifolium grow with the smaller martagon lilies. An usunual crown vetch *Coronilla varia* and other wild and feral plants grow in the grass banks.

The National Trust for Scotland Conservation Volunteers have helped to improve access to the wider estate, cutting back some of the shrubby thugs, and helping with the management of areas of flowering meadow that include wild flowers and others that naturalise readily. Hill of Tarvit is an example of a garden where there is considerable awareness that a garden of horticultural distinction can also function as a significant resource for wildlife. Even the Edwardian borders are maintained to provide shelter and nectar and pollen both on the ground and high up, with the spread upwards and outwards of early- and late-flowering shrubs and trees.

There has been continued monitoring of the garden lawns since nineteen kinds of waxcap fungi (*Hygrocybe*) were discovered to be thriving in some of them. One species *Hygrocybe calyptriformis*, is included in the Red Data Book. It is a ballet-shoe shade of daring glistening pink. Unfortunately, few people in the British Isles have an appreciation of fungi, but hygrocybes are of national and Europe-

wide significance, and encouraging an awareness of them is part of the garden's developing conservation role.

Hill of Tarvit was recently given a substantial hellebore collection. These include some very choice cultivars of the Ballard strain and others from the noted collector Will McLewin. Early to flower, these plants add glamour to the start of the year.

▲ Mullein, yellow rattle, bird's-foot trefoil and orange hawkweed among other wild flowers in the meadow area

117

Hugh Miller's Cottage

Along the Inverness coastline and over to the Black Isle, the drive northwards to the small fishing port of Cromarty has some wonderful views down over the Firth. In Church Street, Cromarty, is the cottage built by Hugh Miller's great-grandfather about 1698. Miller's fame rests on his knowledge of natural history and geology of Scotland, especially that of his native region. Born in 1802, he became a stone-mason, travelling a good deal and becoming more and more interested in the fossils he found in the rock. A deeply religious man and a reformer, he became editor of *The Witness*, the Edinburgh based newspaper of the Free Church of Scotland in 1840, and he also interested himself in collecting folk tales and local culture. Invited to Edinburgh by leading evangelicals, he moved to the city to further his publishing and editorial work, and quickly established an international reputation.

◀◀ Red poppy *Papaver orientale* against the white-washed side wall of the cottage
◀ The side yard with its strip border, looking down to the Church Street

The thatched cottage he grew up in is furnished with some of his own belongings and contains a Hugh Miller reading room. The small garden with its well, behind the cottage, was redesigned in 1995, the upper part furnished with stone and wood benches. Hugh Miller loved trees and was as attentive to the fauna and flora of his native district as he was to its fossils. He could be formidable in his writings and debate, but he would show children playing in the churchyard the algae, lichens and mosses on grave-stones, and the plant life growing around them.

The cottage garden is planted with wild flowers that make an attractively congested flurry of flower and foliage through spring and summer. The idea has been not to feature rarities but to include many of the local wild flowers. In spring there are primroses and cowslips under wild cherry blossom; then herb Robert and woodrush; moving on into summer through red campion, sweet cicely, blue-bells, alkanet and vetches.

A few naturalised plants such as rose of Sharon and lady's mantle join the St John's wort, foxglove and scabious in high summer. It is very pleasant to sit on the sun-dappled raised terrace scented with honeysuckle, at the end of this garden by the cherry and rowan trees and to listen to the birds, looking down over the rest of the garden and the cottage. Hugh Miller himself carved the handsome sundial with an acanthus leaf motif stationed at a curve in the path. The dressed Clasnach sandstone in the courtyard at the front of the cottage is also evidence of Miller's skill as a stonemason.

The adjoining cottage, now the Miller House Museum (opened in 2003) houses a fossil collection and exhibition rooms displaying Hugh Miller's work.

◀ This tiny wild garden is full of dappled shade and native trees and wild flowers

▶ Looking towards the sundial carved by Hugh Miller

▼ The end of the garden with its raised bed, seat and well

He wrote an important and popular book on geology, *Old Red Sandstone*, and made significant discoveries of fossil fish in the local sandstone in Cromarty. Two were named after him: the placoderms *Coccosteus milleri* and *Pterichthys milleri* (later *Coccosteus cuspidatus* and *Pterichthyodes milleri*). He was also interested in folklore and vernacular history and recorded many stories and myths in his books. Behind the museum is a narrow, raised strip sheltered by the far wall and warmed by the sun, for which a garden is planned. Miller was one of the first to recognise that life, like 'a green web', consisted of successive existence and extinction. In these two modest gardens, visitors can be reminded of Hugh Miller's achievements and curiosity about landscape: 'nature always a fresh study'.

Inveresk Lodge
Gardens

The garden at Inveresk Lodge is a place of open brightness, even in overcast weather. The south-facing hillside garden looks out over sloping lawns and generous beds of flowers, shrubs and fine trees, across the flood plain of the River Esk, to the distant Pentland Hills. The village of Inveresk, in East Lothian, six miles east of Edinburgh, is one of the driest areas in Scotland and the soil here is an equable sandy loam.

Through the confines of the stone courtyard, a mature garden landscape of trees, stonework, colour and scent, aprons out before you. The purple tones of the sandstone walls of the Upper Garden are echoed by shrubs such as purple hazel *Corylus avellana* 'Fuscorubra'and hedges of purple cherry plum *Prunus cerasifera* 'Nigra'. The theme continues with alliums and perennials in the island beds, and *Ligularia dentata* 'Desdemona' with its maroon-purple foliage set against a backdrop of *Aralia elata*.

◀◀　*Iris bucharica* at the foot of the stone urn
◀　The 17th-century sundial on the upper lawn

▲ Inveresk has the National Plant Collection of tropaeolums: *Tropaeolum polyphyllum*, *T. tuberosum* var. *lineamaculatum* 'Ken Aslett' and *T. hookerianum* subsp. *hookerianum* pictured above are three of the total of twenty two held here

◀ The garden in autumn, the golden maple *Acer cappadocicum* 'Aureum' on the right

Inverewe Garden

People who know nothing about Scottish gardens have heard of Inverewe. It has come to represent the epitome of west coast gardens, its reputation earned over 140 years of horticultural innovation and development. I have visited many times, mostly seeing it mysteriously cocooned in mist or rain. Once, the sun blazed and the whole garden steamed in the heat of late summer. The herbaceous plants were beginning to droop slightly in the Walled Garden; the scents and colours were stunning. Up at the highest viewpoint, you could hear the gorse popping as its seedpods cracked, ejecting the seeds.

Inverewe more than almost any other garden is layered with the creative effort of a succession of talented gardeners: Osgood Mackenzie, his daughter Mairi Sawyer and the head gardeners of The National Trust for Scotland. Starting in the 1860s, Osgood Mackenzie made the structure of the

◄◄◄ *Primula* 'Inverewe'
◄◄ The vivid *Meconopsis punicea*
◄ The Chilean bellflower *Lapageria rosea*

137

The sweep of the Walled Garden alongside Loch Ewe in winter

garden: the walled kitchen garden on an ancient raised beach curving around the bay of Loch Ewe the shelterbelts protecting the garden – open on three sides to the sea. The rocky outcrop he had chosen was bare and windswept, having been cleared of trees earlier, so he brought soil by boat, for the kitchen garden and for planting plots. His daughter Mairi gardened with her father, and then, after his death in 1922, continued to develop the garden, giving it to The National Trust for Scotland in 1953. She and her architect husband,

built a new house, to replace the former mansion which burned down in 1914. She made a distinctive rock garden below the front lawn of the house. Her token border above the lawn was extended and developed to its present richness by the Trust.

There are plants at Inverewe found nowhere else in the British Isles, and some found hardly anywhere else in the world. The present Head Gardener, John Anderson, has a firm sense of the design of the garden as a whole, and is also a skilled plantsman. He feels it is in the spirit of Inverewe

actively to seek out new plants, quite as much as to preserve the famous introductions of the past. By *Am Plocard* (the High Viewpoint), for example, is one of the few examples of the Tasmanian groundsel tree *Brachyglottis brunonis* growing in Britain, and in the woodland area select plants thrive in the dappled shade under the trees and rhododendrons. The unusual Chinese shrub *Symplocos pyrifolia* which has privet-like foliage, and the rare *Daphniphyllum macropodum*, an East Asian evergreen shrub with scented leaves, are recent plantings.

Several cultivars were raised at Inverewe and named after the garden: the red-orange *Primula* (a *P. cockburniana* hybrid), a hybrid rhododendron, and box, all named 'Inverewe'. The garden holds five National Collections: the New Zealand groundsel trees *Brachyglottis*, the daisy bush *Olearia* and three groups of rhododendrons, subsections *Glischra* and *Maculifera* (mostly from China) and Barbata, which comes from the Himalayas. *Ourisia*, low-growing Australasian and South American plants with dainty tube-shaped flowers, known as New Zealand foxgloves, are also grown at Inverewe. The named cultivars 'Loch Ewe' and 'Snowflake' were raised there.

Warmed by the North Atlantic Drift, this north-western garden harbours plants from temperate rain-forests worldwide. The resin-scented *Cryptocarya alba* originated from Chile and there are the spiky puyas from the high forests of Argentina and Mexico. The madrone *Arbutus menziesii*, with its gloriously cinnamon-coloured trunk, is an eye-catching tree from North America. A variegated Turkey oak *Quercus cerris* 'Argenteovariegata', growing to the northeast of the house, thought to be the finest in the world, was planted by Mairi Sawyer in 1937. Notable plants from Australia and New Zealand include tall leptospermums and several beautiful eucalyptus. In the sunnier conditions of the Walled Garden, the handsome large-leaved *Sparrmannia africana* can, in mild winters, survive outdoors in the Walled Garden, alongside the unusual ginger *Hedychium greenei*, and large and uncommon salvias. This is frankly paradise for a plant enthusiast, but any visitor will appreciate the beautiful harmonies of texture and colour in the plant associations throughout the garden.

The soil at Inverewe is constantly being replenished and enriched with mulches of manure, seaweed and compost made in the garden. The beds and borders are mulched at least once a year, and again if new planting is taking place. The underlying rock is Torridonian sandstone, old and hard enough to build with. The Walled Garden is made of this attractive pink rock.

Although the outer surround of pines, birch, and rowan is continually being renewed, it is no longer accurate to think in terms of shelterbelts as the main protection for the garden. The big trees throughout the garden continuously filter the wind. The great silver firs *Abies alba*, hemlock *Tsuga*, Scots pine and rarer specimen trees such as the southern beech *Nothofagus betuloides* and a Chilean hazel *Gevuina avellana* of record height, are all valued specimens in themselves and large enough to provide necessary shelter for smaller shrub and herbaceous plants below. Sometimes the original planting has not been a success: Lawson cypresses, for example, are too large and cast too much shade, so, as they get damaged or die, they are being replaced by Scots and lodgepole pines. Many plants

▲ *Isoplexis sceptrum* from Madeira
◣ *Xerochrysum subundulatum*
▶ *Ourisia* 'Loch Ewe'

self-seed, griselinias for example and even the New Zealand hoherias, and the scented evergreen *Drimys lanceolata*. This drimys is practically a weed, according to John Anderson, though 'a very nice weed'. *Rhododendron ponticum*, usually considered a pest, he regards as a useful plant – in its place. It makes a dense non-flowering hedge (clipped annually) along the top of the Walled Garden that combs the wind and sea spray, keeping them from the brilliant Mediterranean Border within, with its scented cistus, teuchriums, lavenders and euphorbias.

The weather at Inverewe is the greatest influence

◀ Tasmanian snowgum *Eucalyptus coccifera* in the rock garden
▼ Hydrangea and silver-leaved *Astelia chathamica*

on what grows there. Each year, some trees are damaged or suffer windblow. This may open inviting clearings, or leave plants dangerously exposed to winds. John Anderson accepts 'climate is in control'. He sees his job as responding to the exigencies of climate and weather, dealing with the immediate crises, and planning long term ' exactly as the founder gardeners used to do'.

Inverewe is famous for its rhododendrons. There are well over 2000 different kinds growing there and in addition to the wide Rhododendron Walk, there are the Niveum and the Campylocarpum Walks, named after the particular species planted in them. The garden's founder was nicknamed 'bigleaf' Osgood because of his preference for large-leaved rhododendrons, such as the *sino-grande* and *macabeanum* kinds but subsequent

planting has been inclusive, so Inverewe now has a wide range, flowering at different times of the year. Their showy bloom and foliage combines for effect with other flowering trees such as eucryphias, magnolias, acacia-like lomatias, and herbaceous plants, rather than dominating the garden.

The garden has a large collection of herbaceous plants that enjoy dappled woodland conditions. Alongside west coast specialities such as roscoeas, cardiocrinums and feathery-leaved thalictrums, are wonderfully robust specimens of uncommon plants such as the Madeiran *Isoplexis sceptrum*, which has brown flowerheads, and yellow Korean waxflower *Kirengeshoma palmata* Koreana Group, also called the shuttlecock plant because of the shape of its flowers.

There are no burns at Inverewe, so plants that like wet or waterside conditions, and the ponds and valleys where they grow, depend on rainfall. In one of the damper valleys, rogersias, astilbes and ligularias thrive and the unusual Magellan daisy *Senecio smithii*, recently planted, has done handsomely. Some areas are dry. *Darmera peltata* is one of very few plants that does well in dry shade, and in autumn a long border of this large-leaved plant in the Rhododendron Walk turns deep red contrasting with the gold of the autumnal rowans and the evergreen rhododendrons.

Mairi Sawyer's Rock Garden is dominated by the white, pink and beige-grey multiple trunks of a great Tasmanian snowgum *Eucalyptus coccifera*. Being so close to the shore, this area looks wonderful in the summer season, but gets bombarded by salt-laden winter winds. Some plants such as the silvery-leaved celmisias and the avens genus *Dryas* are tolerant of these sunny windy conditions and do very well here.

The Walled Garden holds a magnificent sweep of

▲ Crocrosmias, agapanthus and galtonias in the hottest part of the Walled Garden
◀ Naturalised dog's-tooth violet *Erythronium revolutum*

vegetables and fruit, below which is an arrangement of borders and beds with a range of herbaceous plants that like more open conditions. In the enclosure towards the eastern end is a tumultuously colourful explosion of bright colour, contrived by the juxtaposition of fiery crocosmias, blue agapanthus, strong coloured gazanias, offset by pale watsonias, the fishing-rod dieramas, and pink tritonias. This brilliant display of rather tender South African perennials makes a tremendous flourish with which to end a walk of the garden in summer.

Kellie Castle

The western part of the garden at Kellie Castle fits neatly in the angle of the castle walls, making the ancient building itself part of the garden vista. From anywhere in the garden you look up towards the high sandstone walls, the skyline of turrets and gables and Ballachulish tiles, and the Renaissance window projecting from the east tower. As you approach the castle, you can, if you scan high on the south-facing wall of the east tower, see the date 1573 and the initials of Margaret Hay who was assigned the estate at Kellie, near Cupar in Fife, as a dower by her husband Lawrence, the 4th Lord Oliphant. The east tower, probably built for her, looks out to the Firth of Forth, and northward to the garden. Part of the north tower is thought to date from 1360, and there may have been an earlier garden, but the age of the garden walls, estimated to be about 400 years, indicates that its present shape derives from the 16th century.

◀◀ Looking towards the castle through galtonia
Galtonia candicans
◀ Scented geraniums in a stone vase sculpted by Hew Lorimer

A glimpse of the Head Gardener through a screen of cordon gooseberries

◀ Hew Lorimer bench with the beautiful, sweet-scented *Rosa* 'Emily Gray' behind

The present garden with its cross axial paths, old rose walks, and box-edged, south-facing vegetable garden was designed by Professor James Lorimer, his young wife Hannah and their six children (Robert Lorimer in particular) who came to a ruinous Kellie in 1878. The roof was missing, not one of its 82 windows had glass, and a local farmer was using the great hall to store grain. The youngest daughter Louise wrote that

> 'it was left to the rooks and owls who built in its scrumbling chimney sand, dropped down piles of twigs which reached out into the rooms . . . every pane of glass was broken and swallows built in the coronets on the ceilings . . .'

The Lorimers had chanced upon Kellie while on holiday in Fife, and it struck a chord. They agreed an 'improving lease' with the owner, The Earl of Mar & Kellie (an old acquaintance of the Professor), that he would make the castle weatherproof, while the family restored the dilapidated interior and garden. It nearly fell into ruin again on the death of John Henry, the Professor's second son, in 1936 but was rescued by the garden-loving Mary MacLeod Wylie and her husband, the sculptor Hew Lorimer, Robert Lorimer's son. After Mary Lorimer's death in 1970 the ownership of Kellie passed to The National Trust for Scotland which has maintained the garden in the Scottish Arts and Crafts style that was so strongly identified with Robert Lorimer's landscape design and architecture. It is recognisably the same garden that you see in the painting made by another son, John Henry Lorimer, in 1916.

History, in the form of royal associations and grim facts of war, death and exile, is built into the fabric of Kellie Castle, but the castle and garden as they are now smile over the surrounding pastures and woodland. It is one of the gentlest and most

'September' a John Henry Lorimer painting of the garden

inviting of all Scottish gardens, full of colour and scent. The proportions seem exactly right for its situation and the economy of the design allows for ornament and embellishment that never seem fussy, such as the central armillary sphere or the stone sculptures of Hew Lorimer. The Walled Garden is not large, about 0.6 hectare, but it has been designed to disclose a succession of views, and internal details of great charm, each area different but coherently part of a whole.

There was an overgrown garden design still visible at Kellie when the Lorimers arrived. Louise described a garden, still encircled by a tumbledown wall, which was a wilderness of neglected gooseberry bushes, gnarled apple trees and old world

147

roses, that struggled through the weeds, summer after summer, with a sweet persistence.

Robert Lorimer and his family respected the old pattern of paths as they developed the design for the new garden which incorporated a main central path, two small corner gardens (Robin's Garden and the Secret Garden) and a neat stone garden house.

The rose-lined Secret Garden, enclosed by yew hedges with an arch threaded with Scottish flame creeper *Tropaeolum speciosum*, contains a sculpture by Robert's son Hew, added later, of a large basket carved in stone (replacing the Cupid in the painting by his uncle, in the drawing room). Hew also made two benches: a three-sectioned corner seat in Robin's Garden, and another, further west, to commemorate the site of an old beech. The two corner gardens are favourite places for many of the garden's resident birds: wrens, blackbirds, and wagtails, and for summer-visiting warblers.

John Lorimer made several smaller paintings of Kellie plants such as roses and the Christmas rose hellebore *Helleborus niger*. There is also a view of the garden from the Vine Room showing the house martins that still nest there each summer. Initially, the Lorimers and the birds shared the house because of the state of the roof when they first moved in. The inscription above the entrance reads 'This mansion snatched from crows and owls is dedicated to honest ease amid labours' (HOC DOMICILIUM CORVIS ET BUBONIBUS EREPTUM HONESTO INTER LABORES OTIO CONSECRATUM EST). CORVIS is sometimes translated as 'rooks', perhaps because they are mentioned in Louise Lorimer's early account, though her description of the birds' behaviour – nest-building in chimneys, dropping twigs into the rooms – is typical of jackdaws, still common at Kellie.

◀ Bee skep in its niche in the garden wall

◀ Looking down the fruit and vegetable border to the Summer House designed by Robert Lorimer

▶ Purple broad beans in flower in the vegetable border

◀ Crown imperial *Fritillaria imperialis* and tulip 'Queen of Night'

▶ Delphiniums

An old wall-trained pear 'Hessle' on the south-facing outside wall

There is a happy mixture of formal structure and informal planting that is particularly appreciated today. To my mind, this garden is a small masterpiece, ahead of its time, avoiding the laborious complexities of Jekyll and the some of the awkwardnesses of Robinson. This was how Robert Lorimer wanted it: 'One enters the walled garden direct out of the house . . . the flowers, fruit and vegetables are all mixed up together.'

A John Henry Lorimer painting of 1892 ('Kellie Castle, Fife 1892') shows white trumpet lilies *Lilium longiflorum*, popular at the time, growing with tall crimson pinks in of one of the borders, and it is no accident that there is a branch of an apple tree hung with ripe fruit framing the upper part of the picture. Fruit trees are trained up the walls through the Walled Garden including a recently planted 'Irish Peach' apple. Outside on the terrace walls a 100-year-old Scots pear 'Hessle' still bears fruit.

Gertrude Jekyll wrote approvingly about Kellie in *Some English Gardens* (sic) published in 1904. She mentions walks with box edgings and 'quantities of simple flowers', selecting for special attention: Shirley poppies, tall snapdragons, columbines, meadowsweet, lilies and good strains of single and double hollyhocks (all pictured in George Elgood's painting in the book). She remarks on 'Scotch briers and other roses' in a general sort of way, 'in close companionship with other strong-growing plants'. Robert Lorimer recalled meeting Gertrude Jekyll early in his career but it is uncertain whether she ever visited Kellie. Elgood, a keen gardener himself, supplied Miss Jekyll with notes for this book.

An intimate and knowledgeable first-hand account of the Kellie roses by Louise Lorimer survives in an essay in which she evaluates a range of individual kinds and named varieties to light on 'one perfect rose'; she finally decides it would be the "Blush China" (now known as old blush China) which grows still on the outside of the terrace wall at Kellie,

flowering faithfully . . . from May to November. Lavishly, graciously, it flowers with a wealth of true pink blossoms shading to deeper buds, with its polished dark green leaves, its sturdy growth, its delicious scent which haunts the petals even when they have fallen.

Other China roses, some now quite rare, that were in Louise's Victorian collection still grow at Kellie. They include Fortune's double yellow and the lovely pink semi-double 'Madame Laurette Messimy', and flourish alongside those that have remained favourites such as 'Madame Alfred Carrière', 'Gloire de Dijon' and 'Cécile Brünner'. The Ayrshire ramblers and scramblers are well represented, as are some of the delightful old Penzance sweetbriars that Louise loved. She was also enthusiastic about the new vigorous *R. wichurana* hybrid climbers that carried bloom late in the season, such as 'Jersey Beauty' and 'Sanders White Rambler'.

The Trust restoration keeps a focus on the late Victorian Lorimer rose collection, grown in a variety of ways here; there are shrubs large and small in borders and, where paths cross, some bushes with hooped supports, which enable you to see the blooms of types such as *Rosa* 'Alba Maxima' to best advantage. 'Gallica' and 'Celeste' roses are pruned into old-style hedges. Others such as 'Rambling Rector' climb into old damson trees and up the warmest walls. Rugosas 'F.J. Grootendorst', 'Blanc Double de Coubert' and 'Roseraie de l'Hay' arch out of borders, and 'Félicité Perpétue' and 'American Pillar' are densely snaked up and over the arches. Later introductions include 'Albertine', 'Etoile de Hollande' and 'Emily Gray'. A nice ruse, introduced by a previous Head Gardener, was to weave sweet peas up older roses that had become a little leggy.

The main vista to the armillary sphere has to be glamorous, planted with the exuberant nepeta *Nepeta* x *faassenii* backed by tall purple blue delphiniums or creamy galtonias *Galtonia candicans* and gorgeous hedges of the apothecary's rose *Rosa gallica* var. *officinalis*.

Vegetable beds, grown organically inside an edging of box, run along the south-facing, north wall in a bold sweep that was daring in Edwardian times and in some respects is still. For though potagers have become fashionable over the past few decades, they are usually separate from the purely ornamental areas of the garden. At Kellie this south-facing vegetable border is clearly an integrated part of the whole, and here you can really appreciate the beauty of the foliage and flowers of food plants well grown.

Tomatoes and potatoes, members of the *Solanaceae*, a family that contains many ornamentals, are handsome in flower and foliage. Kellie grows Scottish potato varieties such as the unusual 'Edzell

Blue', 'Shetland Black', 'Arran Victory' and 'British Queen', 'Arran Beauty', 'Dunbar Rover' and 'Dunbar Standard'. Modern varieties especially those bred for growing without heavy doses of pesticide (such as 'Appell', 'Cara', 'Cosmos', 'Osprey', 'Premier' and 'Valour'), are also grown. They do well here in the sandy soil with enough silt content to give structure, but the ground is regularly mulched with organic compost and composted cow manure.

Against the stone of the walls the plants, including the trained fruit trees, look their best. It is a treat also to see the sun shine though the handsome foliage of 'Brown Golding', an old kind of lettuce, or on broad beans in blossom. It is easy to see why runner beans were grown as ornamentals before their usefulness as a green vegetable was accepted. Many of the plants, such as the tall pea 'Duke of Albany' and a good number of the potatoes and other plants, are 'Heritage' varieties, of Scottish origin where possible.

All gardens change. At Kellie, Sinclair Williamson, the Head Gardener respects the past while introducing new plants and ideas 'in a way that fits in with the overall sense of the place'. The sunny garden house with its 'Arts and Crafts' bird-like motif, now houses a pictorial history of the garden. Robin's Corner, favourite spot of Robert Lorimer (known as Robin as a child) is being replanted with new roses, including Scotch briars and 'White Pet'. A new corner garden of ferns and snowdrops where the gardener's hut used to be, is entered through a trellis arch hung with the *Rosa filipes* 'Kiftsgate'.

The castle and its garden have managed to keep the intimacy of a family home. Somehow it still feels lived in – or at least inhabited by – people who love it. Sit in the friendly tearoom scented by fresh-picked *Rosa gallica* and marigolds on the table; the food is good and homemade and you look out over the Firth of Forth and feel like a welcome house guest.

A different scarecrow is made each year by the children of the local school

Leith Hall

The Leiths were a prosperous family of some standing as long ago as the 14th century. They were shippers in Edinburgh with connections and property reaching some distance up into the northeast. In 1650, James Leith built the attractive country house named for his family, on land bought by his father at Kennethmont, 36 miles northwest of Aberdeen. The early garden for this house is shown on General Roy's map c.1750 as a rectangular enclosure around the house and another wooded enclosure further up the hillside to the northeast.

Research over the past few years, has shown that the garden landscape of Leith Hall has grown incrementally from the founding of the estate to the present day. Survey drawings made in the mid-18th century, and plans drawn up in 1797 by George Brown, the estate surveyor at Gordon Castle – who also made the review of Craigievar Castle – give us

◀◀ The vista over the zigzag border and the outside of the walled garden, over the woodlands
◀ Gardeners' garters grass with a self-sown form of the golden daisy *Anthemis tinctoria*

The daisy saltires, a simple idea beautifully put into effect by differential mowing

a good idea of its direction. They show the house remodelled and enlarged, now focused on a larger east wing and a series of formal gardens extending north, up the hillside. The existing semicircular stable building was constructed in 1754 with a garden, as at present, to the east. The plan shows another, mirror-image stable, with a formal garden below it but there is no evidence that either was built.

The 17th and 19th lairds, both distinguished soldiers, General Alexander Leith-Hay, 1758-1838, and his grandson of the same name, 1818-1900, continued extending both house and garden during the 19th century. (Hay was added to the name in respect of a generous great uncle who had endowed the house with much-needed money.) In the early years of the century, a prosperous period for Aberdeenshire, and also for the estate of Leith Hall,

the park was planted with trees. A semi-circle of shrubs around the stable block and East Garden next to it was given paths, a triangle of shrubs and fruit trees along the east and west perimeter paths.

When Colonel Alexander Leith-Hay returned to Scotland in 1860, he extended and elaborated the East Garden, probably built the wall bounding it and added the splendid glasshouses, forming the basis of the designed landscape as we know it today. A survey of the time details seventy significant parkland trees, mostly broadleaves, with a dozen or so conifers.

Charles Edward Leith-Hay, who succeeded his uncle in 1900, and his wife Henrietta, dominated the 20th-century history of the estate. Charles designed the wrought iron main entrance gates with their monogrammed initials, and the gates to the new West Garden, all made by a local blacksmith.

Henrietta gave the estate to The National Trust for Scotland in 1945, but continued to live in the house, and to exert an influence over the garden. She died in 1965, and her niece The Hon. Mary O'Neill known as Midi, with her husband Lieutenant Colonel Derick Gascoigne continued as tenants, and restored part of the garden that had been used as for market gardening during the Second World War. Their son and his wife continue as tenants of the north wing.

Charles and Henrietta initiated many of the characteristic features of the gardens. The best-known is the Moon Gate, built into the north wall. To reach it, you pass two ancient stones, thought to be Pictish, one with a carved image of a salmon, the other of a wolf. Semicircular steps sweep impressively to the elegant wrought-iron railings of the gate itself, creating a high, round window with a glimpse to the rocky hillside rising behind it. There is a road close by, but it is invisible from the garden.

This Moon Gate. unlike its Chinese model, is more an attribute of the garden below, than a window into to a wider landscape. The plants in the borders by the Moon Gate include several from China including the formidable *Rosa sericea R.* subsp. *omeiensis pteracantha* with its white cruciform flowers and huge, translucently scarlet, winged thorns. The visitor does not feel a strong invitation to climb the steps; this is a piece of architecture to admire. There is another purpose at work here. The Moon Gate draws you to this high northerly point in the garden, to marvel; this accomplished, you turn back – to catch your breath at the best views of Leith Hall, southwards over the garden. From here the eye can rove into the distant landscape beyond: east towards Bennachie, along the Coreen Hills to Tap o' Noth behind the treeline in the west.

The zigzag border is another of Charles' and Henrietta's star enterprises. The Leith Hall twists are there not of necessity, as in the case of the 18th-century paths that zigzagged walkers up steep

▲ The Moon Gate
◀ *Rosa* 'Cantabrigiensis' a lovely rose hybridised at Cambridge Botanic Gardens from the golden Rose of China, *R. xanthina* f. *hugonis*

Stone cougar one of a pair crouched on top of the wall by the garden gates

wooded hangers, but a device taking the eye to different views as you proceed. The open side has a superb high-season Scots border with great clumps of giant meadowsweet *Filipendula rubra* 'Venusta' which is pink and creamy, and *Filipendula camtschatica* both growing up to 3 metres in height, with *Filipendula purpurea* and joe-pye weed about half that size. In the 1900s, chrysanthemums grew opposite in the wall border. Later, there were plums, but in recent years its fame has rested on the tremendous flow of colour composed entirely of two kinds of catmint (*Nepeta* x *faassenii* and 'Six Hills Giant').

A bold rock garden designed by Charles Leith-Hay, was made in the 1920s to crown a hillside to the west of the house, rising to 624 feet about sea level. Photographs taken between 1929 and 1955 show a formidable piece of work; the rocks, artfully arranged, towering over the paved paths and steps, with plants of all kinds growing on and among them. A letter from Brian Gascoigne in 1975 noted the plant rarities here and 'an interesting and unusual, imaginatively laid-out collection of alpines in and out of

some largish rock, beautifully proportioned . . . made over a lifetime by Henrietta Leith-Hay'.

The Trust redesigned this garden (not then recognised as significant) with low-maintenance heathers and conifers, and with frugality rather than history or aesthetics in mind. The rock garden which was previously dynamic, depending for its effect on the cascades of plants such as yellow alyssum, aubrieta, phloxes, saxifrages and campanulas, was toned down and many of its rocks moved away despite the anguish of Midi Gasgoigne (Henrietta Leith-Hay's niece). 'I know the work has to be simplified but would it have not been possible to leave those great stones placed there by Charles Leith-Hay and forming a rock garden of quite unusual boldness, vision and naturalness?' The south side of the rock garden was simplified between the mid-1960s and 1986 when The Scottish Rock Garden Club replanted the much smaller, redesigned space.

Times change, and if there is regret for the loss of the drama and coherence of the original rock garden, and the rock border which led back to the East Garden, the best is made of the rock plants and pools and the features that remain. There are two spiky New Zealand aciphyllas, silvery celmisias and hard cushions of *Azorella trifurcata*. A succession of primroses of different colour and form flower from spring through to autumn including *Primula prolifera* and *Primula florindae*.

In the adjacent Fern Garden variations of *Dryopteris* species, the large royal fern *Osmunda regalis* and different forms of hart's-tongue *Asplenium scolopendrium* grow with exotics such as the Japanese painted fern *Athyrium niponicum* var. *pictum*. Huge-leaved *Gunnera manicata*, the dwarf willow *Salix lanata*, and Chilean bamboos are interspersed among the ferns, and the boundary of the garden is marked by *Spiraea veitchii*.

The eastward path, edged by shrub borders, includes an interesting display of deutzias and philadelphus, including *Philadelphus purpurascens* whose great charm lies in its scented, white single flowers that contrast with the purple calyx. This border also has a good show of herbaceous plants including *Podophyllum hexandrum*.

The large Walled Garden is subdivided many times, the current Head Gardener, using innovative techniques to introduce new ideas sympathetic to the garden's history, and where possible and feasible, putting back some of the old landmarks – such as fruit trees – destroyed during the 1938-45 market-garden period. The suite of impressive glasshouses was taken down between 1956-1971. Part of the wall describing its roofline, its steps and paving remain, cascading with hardy geraniums and rock plants, and ornamented with urns, replicating those that used to stand here.

The Rose Garden is a mixture of some of the hardier old-fashioned and modern shrub roses, chosen to withstand the northerly latitude, gusting winds and altitude. They are underplanted with columbines, alliums and violas. Another section of the Walled Garden has climbing 'New Dawn' roses trained through a stout wooden gazebo. The darker pink 'Albertine' drapes itself along a rustic fence.

The southern part of the garden contains an east-facing border, and some beautiful young trees, including the paperbark maple *Acer griseum* but its main feature is a simple but dramatic daisy-filled quadruple saltire cut out in grass. The differential mowing continues downhill, cut in a tapering cone and narrowing downhill to the focal point of the gateway beyond. Beyond the Moon Gate, the 18th-century stables on the eastern boundary of the garden are the inspiration for a circle of trees, within which is a grass spiral maze planted with spring bulbs.

The landscape around Leith House, described in the late 18th century as 'superior to most' having 'southerley exposure, fertile soil . . . well sheltered' is a good place to grow plants. Older trees such as the caramel-scented *Cercidiphyllum japonicum* are very fine, and newer planting, such as the dawn redwood *Metasequoia glyptostroboides*, grows away quickly. The borders race to their summer perfection once the cold weather clears in late spring, with little interference from pests (temperatures range from a hot summer +29° to -23° Celsius in winter). The garden is blissfully disease-free. Its present-day area is nearly 3 hectares, and there are park and woodland walks with wild flowers, such as wood anemones, and ponds with yellow flags, meadow-sweet and waterlilies. Every room of the house has a view over parkland, trees or garden alive with garden and woodland birds.

Looking up the zigzag double border, with its river of nepeta faced by a rich mix of herbaceous plants opposite

Lochalsh Woodland Garden

A massive pine stump and roots, removed from an area due to be flooded makes a feature in the garden at Lochalsh

This garden, spread peacefully alongside Loch Alsh, is part of the larger landscape of the 2550-hectare Balmacara Estate that occupies the western end of the Lochalsh peninsula. Walking through this woodland garden with its old pines, with the water lapping against the great slanting sandstone rocks of the loch shore, it is much like being in one of the great temperate rainforest parks of the Pacific Rim. The illusion is fostered by the presence of Canadian plants, such as the dwarf cornel *Cornus canadensis* among the heathers as you first step into the garden and the pines growing right down to the loch. Lochalsh is a naturalistic and tranquil garden of woods and sea, with view out to Skye and Kintail, and the company of seabirds, and, if you are very fortunate, otters and deer.

The belt of trees that provides shelter for the woodland garden was planted about 1887, probably at the same time that Balmacara House (now a youth hostel and dive centre) was built by Sir Hugh Innes. Having purchased the estate from Seaforth Mackenzie he established a house and was the first landlord to make Lochalsh his home. His great niece and her husband, Isaac William Lillingstone, turned the house into a free hospital. Balmacara Estate was left to The National Trust for Scotland by Lady Margaret MacKinnon Hamilton in 1946, and Lochalsh House and garden came into its care in 1953. Euan Cox, a notable plant collector, was given permission by the Trust to make a woodland garden. He planted *Rhododendron protistum*, and other large-leaf types.

Euan Cox sited his tender rhododendrons in sheltered places amongst the existing Scots pine, oak, larch and beech. The garden is now best known for the *Maddenia* subsection of rhododendrons, which are difficult to grow outdoors in the British Isles. Originating from Himalayan Tibet, Burma, and China, they like cool, sheltered conditions and high humidity, though they are not particular about soil and will grow in limestone

A path winding through the woodland close to the loch

appropriate niches in which to establish the ferns. There are several of the *Dryopteris* genus. Golden male fern *D. affinis*, is a native that grows especially well in west-coast Scotland, and there is a tall hybrid *D. x complexa* 'Stablerae' which has narrow, ruffled fronds. Lochalsh also grows the pretty Japanese red shield fern *D. erythrosora* which has bronzed and pink early fronds, and the Indian *D. darjeelingensis* and several other species. *Woodwardia martineẕii*, from the highlands of central Mexico, has been established and there are several native and exotic examples of the dainty maidenhair ferns (*Adiantum* species). There are also some weird and wonderful forms of lady fern *Athyrium filix-femina*.

There is natural regeneration of rowan, holly, birch and some oak within the woodland, but the outer shelterbelt is being actively replanted as trees age or become damaged. The best specimens of rhododendron, eucalyptus and other significant trees (mostly from South America and the Himalaya) growing in the calm areas within the wood, are also being propagated and replanted.

Lochalsh Woodland Garden is set within a landscape of ancient Scottish agriculture. The pre-historic settlements situated nearby are still evident. The agricultural landscape retains the texture of the rural past, with crofting still carried on in parts of the estate. The garden with its unobtrusive woodland tracks is a delight to be in, and long-haul walkers can link up with designated walks in other parts of this large estate. There are many birds including seabirds, and woodland birds such as goldcrests. On a quiet day there is the possibility of seeing a pine marten, and it is a wonderful treat to come across sweeps of lady's tresses orchids *Spiranthes spiralis* in large drifts around some of the upper paths.

or (as predominantly in Scotland) more acid conditions. Some, such as *Rhododendron maddenii* subsp. *crassum* are beautifully scented.

The long drive to Lochalsh House (not open to the public) is planted with fuchsias, and the attractive garden below the house has herbaceous borders and hydrangeas. Close to the nearby Coach House, used as offices by the Trust, is another more intensively gardened space, hedged on the shore side with bamboo. Above is a small bamboo garden, and bamboos are planted in naturalistic clumps further up the hillside.

Ferns grow naturally in this woodland and many non-native cultivars have been planted with them, but so skilfully that they look completely at home. In order to create this natural impression, gardeners and volunteers laboured hard, climbing the woodland slopes with supplies of rocks and soil, making

▲ Spring, lily-flowered tulips (a batch supplied in error and so far unidentified)
▶ Autumn with *Sorbus* 'Joseph Rock'

Malleny Garden

A country garden only six miles southwest of the city centre of Edinburgh, Malleny is nestled into a hillside sheltered from the winds by a belt of woodland. It is a quiet, reflective garden, full of roses and informal borders brimming with campanulas, day lilies, tall herbs and striking trees, enclosed within old walls and hedges. Neither grand nor sensational, it is cherished by the city's garden-lovers, and visitors come over and again.

Just beyond the stone wall to the northwest, runs the Bavelaw Burn. Summer visitors walking by the low path hear the sound of the water as they enjoy the scents of the roses for which this garden is celebrated. Nineteenth-century Rambler roses such as 'Félicité Perpétue' climb the walls. Damasks 'De Rescht' and 'La Ville de Bruxelles' and the Noisette 'William Allen Richardson' of the same period interweave through a happy combination of other roses, shrubs and larger perennials in the generous borders. Malleny Gardens holds the National Plant Collection of 19th-century shrub roses, which attracts connoisseur rosarians worldwide, in high summer.

◀ A bush of spignel *Meum athamanticum*, an aniseed-scented herb used to flavour snuff

▶ Paeonies thrive at Malleny; these are 'Bowl of Beauty'

◀ Nasturtiums and sweet peas intertwine with the colours and textures of the vegetables in the raised beds of the potager

▶ The paths are now made from local whinstone which blends softly with the yew arches and hedges and the tumult of shrub roses – here 'Président de Sèze' and 'Buff Beauty'

It is a place of intimacy and seclusion and has been so for a long time. Maps from the mid-19th century show a garden structurally much as it is now, with its centrally bisecting yew hedge and trees. Photographs from just before the Second World War show a garden with the same principal features: abundant roses, fine trees, wide borders, yews, neatly clipped hedges and lawns.

The earliest records of the garden go back to 1330 with a house on the site from about 1594. The present attractive but modest country house was built about 1635 for Sir James Murray of Kilbaberton. The four great clipped yew trees that dominate the upper garden are also believed to date from the 17th century. The house acquired a wing in the Georgian style in 1823, and the lawn by this part of the house is dominated by a magnificent deodar cedar, probably planted shortly after the building work was finished.

The garden is fairly high at 500 feet above sea level and predominantly north-facing but sheltered, trapping the sun in summer and holding on to its snow cover in winter. Red Moss, one of the largest raised bogs in Midlothian lies to the south, and beyond it rise the Pentland Hills.

The views at Malleny are inward and contemplative, but not shut in. It has a strong structure of paths, walls and hedges that create a space of dynamic balance rather than strict geometry. Nothing in the garden is perfectly symetrical. The entrance gate, with its handsome ironwork, is not quite aligned with the path to the four yews, the ground slopes down towards the burn. To the west, the garden funnels out to another long boundary wall. Only if you look carefully does it strike you that the paths are unequal, and this asymmetry has the effect of making the garden seem larger than it actually is, and slightly mysterious.

On rare occasions the Bavelaw Burn along the boundary swells with excessive rainfall, and sweeps the silt away, scouring the rock of the riverbed so it gleams like bone. This burn is an important wildlife corridor for plants and animals, linking the uplands of the Pentland Hills and the lower Water of Leith valley with the central urban area of Edinburgh.

The rock beneath the garden is sandstone and the soil is light and requires regular feeding. A good deal of mushroom compost is applied, but as is the way in such poorly structured, light, sandy soil, quickly disappears, its nutrients taken up by plants or washed out. Plants such as hostas that are eaten by snails in heavier soils, grow large and unblemished at Malleny but their soil requires regular feeding.

The light soil is good for herbs such as chives, parsleys, sage and thymes which flourish in the herb and ornamental vegetable garden, companioned by nasturiums, tagetes and sweet peas. Some of the larger herbs such as fennels, artemisias, hyssop and lovage are also grown in the borders, providing a handsome foil for roses and shrubs.

The vegetable and herb potager is one of the most recent and popular features of the garden. A clever design (by Yvonne Deacon) of a double pattern of squares and rectangles and triangular beds edged with granite setts, disguises its irregularities. The plants in the outside beds, such as fennel, borage, marjoram, hyssop and dill represent culinary herbs, with valerian and tansy for medicinal uses, and madder as a dye plant. The dry siliceous soil provides a good base for a rare feathery umbellifer called spignel *Meum athamanticum* which used to be used to flavour snuff and foodstuffs. The roots were chewed as an aid to digestion in the Scottish Highlands. It makes a good showing at Malleny where it self-seeds liberally.

▲ Pruning time for the yews to the front of the house (no longer there) in 1928

▼ Present-day view of the yews, through the wrought-iron side gate

Terracotta chimney pots planted with nasturtiums, placed in the centre of each section of the potager, and several attractive openweave basketware globes, give height and focus to the design, especially out of season. Blue cabbages, runner and French beans, leeks, lettuces, chicory and other vegetables are planted in rotation each year, with contrasting areas of tall sweet pea wigwams, the scented perennial honesty *Lunaria rediviva*, white echinops and roses.

Foliage makes an important contribution, especially early and late in the year. The inky dark evergreen of yew is supplemented by the purples of berberis and of the purple-leaved forms of hazel and weigela. The yellow-leaved hostas and variegated London pride provide bright points throughout the growing season, even in dull weather. Foliage provides

▶ The path in the northeast corner of the garden curves between the yew quartet to the Edwardian greenhouse
▼ Malleny House and garden with the woodland to the south on the first edition Ordnance Survey map of 1895

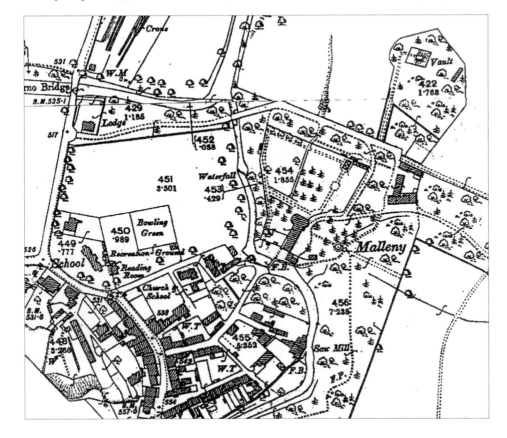

▶ A path through roses, hardy geraniums and a supporting cast of herbaceous plants

▶ *R.* x *harisonii* 'Harison's Yellow', the yellow rose of Texas, with the hardy geranium *G. clarkei* 'Kashmir White'
▶▶ The garden with *Inula hookeri* in the foreground

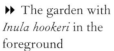

texture as well as colour: the green velvet leaves of the alchemillas, the grey-white origami of artemisia and the silver-grey plush of the peppermint-scented *Pelargonium tomentosum*. This scented-leaf geranium thrives in the fine, dry soil which gives it the best conditions for developing its rich peppermint scent.

Roses provide the strongest scents from mid-summer onwards and herbs such as hyssop, lavender and rosemary play their part, as do larger shrubs including an unusual sorbaria *Sorbaria kirilowii* which produces a mist of sweet-scented white spiraea-like flowers. Later in the year, different kinds of buddleja contribute their various honey scents. Bees and other insects love the herbs and late summer plants. Along the wide north border the late season goes out ablaze with yellow-golds of golden rod, heleniums and inula.

The clipped yews that make a centrepiece to the upper garden are four that remain from a long-ago planting of twelve (the Twelve Apostles), perhaps in the 17th-century garden. Eight were moved near-er the house and to flank the drive, but they grew so large they were cut down in 1963 to allow more light into the house. The paths beneath the remain-ing group of four have had to be enlarged several times to take account of the new growth. Every other year in late August, the Head Gardener gets to grips with clipping these great 10-metre yew cones, which takes an entire week. Philip Deacon, who has been Head Gardener since 1985, has noted a perceptible increase in girth. He keeps the height to 10 metres since this is the maximum reach of the fully extended hydraulic lift he uses – 'It's a long, steady job, but worth it for the views alone.'

The renovated Victorian greenhouse (not quite on the axis of the path) contains a magnificent 'Black Hamburg' ('Schiava Grossa') grapevine and terracotta pots of pelargoniums, scented-leaf gera-

niums, heliotropes, fuchsias and begonias. It also provides a place to overwinter these and other plants that are not hardy through the winter.

Opposite the house, a small, round pool with a trickling fountain fed by a stream is circled lushly with hostas. From here a short flight of steps invites you to mount to a wide, grassy ride and the wood-land beyond.

▲ The graceful line of the early 19th-century part of Malleny House behind *Rosa gallica* var. *officinalis* and *Verbascum chaixii* 'Album'

◀ The stream-fed fountain trickles into a hosta-edged pool, with royal fern to the side

167

Newhailes

▲ Entrance of the ruined 18th-century Shell Grotto
◀ Local people use Newhailes for recreation throughout the year.

The mansion at Newhailes is a historic treasure, subtly conserved by The National Trust for Scotland to earn a Europa Nostra Conservation Award in 2003. The 35 hectares of overgrown parklands and woods that surround the house, and which are conceptually an integral part of Newhailes, also came to the Trust. An archaeological survey of the grounds, coupled with documentary research, indicated that they, too, held secrets from the 18th century. It now seems that Newhailes could be one of the most important designed landscapes in Scotland, concealing in the remnants of its fabric the developments in taste over a century of huge intellectual change. It was a focus for the Scottish Enlightenment. Samuel Johnson (not much given to complimenting Scots) reputedly called the library 'the most learned room in Europe'.

Newhailes embodied the Enlightenment in its inspiration, its architecture and the design of its landscape. A well-appointed but modest Palladian villa was built in 1686 by the Scottish architect James Smith who, because of an investment mishap, had to sell it. In 1709 the estate was bought and

◀ Much of the garden is over grown with ivy and wild flowers, as here around the plinth that used to support one of the two magnificent sphinxes. The landscape has considerable wildlife importance. Flocks of curlew feed in the Sheep Park, the large area just below the terrace, and buzzards overfly the substantial woodlands. Dippers have been seen in the burn, and showy moths, such as elephant hawkmoth and several moth rarities, have been recorded in the woodland that overlies the old water garden.

◀ Wood anemone *Anemone nemorosa* and foxglove *Digitalis purpurea*

renamed Newhailes (after the ruined Hailes Castle near East Linton, owned by his family) by David Dalrymple, later Solicitor General for Scotland. A wealthy Edinburgh lawyer, he wanted a fine country mansion in which to house his superb collection of books. He and his son James greatly enlarged the house, building a remarkable two-storey library that occupied the whole of a new east wing in 1718. A west wing, containing state rooms, was added about 1730. Under James' son, David, Lord Hailes, Newhailes was at the hub of the Scottish Enlightenment. Hailes suggested the idea of biography to Boswell, and commented on Hume's works, while Johnson described Hailes' own *Annals* as a work of '. . . carefully sifted facts, which tells all that is wanted and all that is known, but without any laboured splendour of language . . .' The philosopher David Hume and Adam Smith came to Newhailes, and James Boswell as well as Johnson visited.

The activity of the house extended to the grounds and Newhailes is now thought to have been one of the first intellectually cohesive landscape gardens in Britain. Walking there today, among the derelict remains, there is something about the spatial relationships between the paths, open fields and woods, that connects you with the intense cultural activity that characterised the Edinburgh region in the 18th century.

General Roy's map shows the estate in the mid-18th century, with its characteristic flask-like shape (on a more or less north-south axis) with an avenue of trees leading to the house at the bottom of the neck, just as it opens out into a circular bulb. The gardens immediately to the north are cut with a grid of radiating paths through woodland, and a tree-lined walkway (later known as Ladies' Walk) crosses the Sheep Field, or 'the big field in front of the house'. The woods planted around the margins

▲ The old flower garden to the east of the house (before 1945)

◀ The 1798 Robert Bauchop map of the whole estate of Newhailes

▲ The north entrance of the house *c.*1900
◀ Miss Alice Mary Dalrymple, aged 22 at the garden gate *c.* 1906

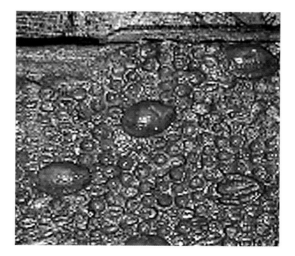

give the estate an impression of even greater extent. Later in the century, the woodland paths by the house were simplified and an open area to the east became an enclosed cabinet garden. It was also, at one time a bowling green.

Newhailes has a burn running through it, which, in the forefront of fashion, was remodelled in the 1740s to make cascades and other waterworks. There are few obvious signs of this now, but part of an elaborate stone-built teahouse remains straddling the water. Later the flow was diverted into a series of culverts, glades and pools with little bridges, no longer visible, but which call out for more

◀ A 2-metre panel from the grotto with impressions of shells, found in the burn in 2003

investigation. In 2003 a plank, still studded with the impressions of shells was found in the water, probably from the Shell Grotto, which was built in the 1760s, and resplendently decorated with native and exotic shells, semi-precious stones and pieces of glass and porcelain. The floor of polished marble and sandstone survives. During the excavations remains of a small three-tiered cascade, possibly a *nymphaeum* was disclosed, but has been covered up again until overall plans for conservation are in place. There are remains of the ice house and another grotto. A large, overgrown, brick-walled garden built just to the southwest of the house has its own puzzlements in the form of large but shallow niches set into some of the walls.

The 500-metre raised terrace known as Ladies' Walk was a feature on the Beauchop map of 1798, where it appears to lead to the chapel on the northern margin of the park. It is well built of stone and remains a riddle; there is nothing quite as extensive elsewhere. Raised walks in 18th-century gardens were usually placed so as to afford a view for the walkers, and the one at Newhailes ended in a platform overlooking Fisherow Harbour and the Forth.

Photographs from the early 1900s show elaborate flower gardens to the west of the house, visible from the state appartments. There are box-edged flowerbeds in cut-out shapes with roses, arches and elegant wrought-iron benches. Seeing the wild and overgrown area that once held these jewel-like beds that demanded so much care and cultivation, is warning enough against hubris in garden-making. The Dalrymples changed the approach to the house from north to south in the 1740s. They made a large north terrace with statues, including two sphinxes grand enough to be noted on the 1909 Ordnance Survey map. The statuary has gone now, but the south-facing frontage is still impressive.

The south side of Newhailes from the flower garden about 1900

Honouring its time of greatest historical and cultural significance, the Dalrymple family behaved as respectful custodians of their family home, hardly changing its 18th-century fabric. Christian Dalrymple, who was chatelaine of Newhailes between 1792 and 1832, added the monumental stables buildings, that are now the Trust offices. Her father explicitly left the property to her and matrilineal heirs thereafter.

The Trust, following the Dalrymple example, has rehabilitated rather than restored the house, repairing its fabric, rather than renewing or replacing it. There is a sense of history throughout, but homeliness also, a kind of domestic rococco. Repairing and refurnishing the house and securing the future of Newhailes, required huge funding, and any kind of restoration of the designed landscape will also be expensive. Further combined archaeological and documentary research will be needed; so at this stage work on the paths and other light maintenance is being carried out, but nothing irreversible is taking place until there is a better sense of the whole.

▲ The Pineapple above the crab apple trees

Since its restoration in the late 1970s, images of the Pineapple, the extraordinary folly in Dunmore Park, just north of Airth near Falkirk, have been so much in the public eye that, when you actually see it, the response is not so much astonishment as a friendly recognition. It is just like its pictures, but more solid and more beautifully carved. Constructed by the 4th Earl of Dunmore, in 1761 the pineapple is 14 metres high, on top of a graceful octagonal tower. This is no light joke; it is a folly of epic proportions.

The first glimpses come as you enter the walled garden, obliquely by a gate in its southeast corner. An orchard of crab apple trees patterns the grassy slopes and the pineapple is just visible over the trees. It is centred in the north wall, mounted on top of a Palladian pavilion of six rooms, constructed so as to form part of the wall. A dainty strip of border that runs just inside the walls skirts the perimeter path that leads up to the edifice. It is a contrast to the traditional Scottish border, typically about 2 metres deep and massed with flowers. Here, a different kind of appreciation is required: you

proceed, noting the character of individual plants, admiring an unusual copper-brown *Rudbeckia hirta* 'Cherokee Sunset', a gladiolus flower and its long spear leaves, and a greeny eucomis flowerhead that echoes, on a small scale, the shape of the pineapple. The effect is one of great charm.

Considered in its historical and cultural context, the giant pineapple has a significance beyond the bizarre. Pineapples came to Europe's attention at the end of the 15th century after Columbus and his crew encountered them, having put to shore in Guadeloupe. Curiosity about the new fruit, and the desire to taste and to grow it, spread through the great houses. The aristocracy vied with each other to bring exotic fruits to perfection, and the pineapple resisted cultivation in a temperate climate longer than most. By the mid-18th century, it was possible – though not easy – to grow pineapples in hothouses. Serving pineapple at table brought credit to its growers, and this, together with the fruit's distinctive shape and symmetry, led to its adoption as an architectural symbol of hospitality and welcome. So this Stirlingshire pineapple,

The Pineapple

mounted upon its attractively proportioned Palladian pavilion, is a fitting emblem for the summer retreat of the 4th Earl, and for present-day holiday visitors who can rent the building from the Landmark Trust. Oddly, despite its fame, the Pineapple's designer is so far unknown. The 6.5-hectare estate was given to The National Trust for Scotland in 1974 by the Countess of Perth.

This walled garden is beautifully built, with high double-skinned brick walls, faced with stone on the north side which used to be the main entrance, the drive led from the former Stirling Road through an avenue of giant redwoods planted by the Earl. It is now bereft of its suite of glasshouses – and therefore of any possibility of growing pineapples – but you can see the marks on the ground and walls where they once stood. Four faux vases disguise chimneys on the pavilion wall that used to vent the furnace that circulated hot air through the cavities in the walls of the summerhouse. Along the east wall, there are some puzzling slots on the walls which may relate to supports for the protection of bygone wall fruits.

Another enclosed garden lies adjacent to the east. It has not yet been restored and awaits an architectural survey. The part-time Head Gardener manages the tumult of wild-flower weeds by simply mowing a sinuous path. In late summer the sea of rosebay is crested in places by robust plants such as crocosmia, the hardy fuchsia *Fuchsia magellanica*, Canadian goldenrod and yellow potentilla; a complete contrast to the orderly orchard next door.

Both gardens are enclosed within a woodland shelterbelt which has itself become the subject of attention. It consists of alder, elm, horse chestnut and *Rhododendron ponticum*. You hear the sound of rooks from the nearby rookery and the occasional mew of buzzards. There is a pond which gives refuge to water figwort *Scrophularia auriculata*, goldilocks or celery-leaved buttercup *Ranunculus sceleratus* and great crested newts. A dipping platform was constructed in 2004 and schools will be invited to do practical work here to learn about their local wildlife.

Pitmedden Garden

Pitmedden, an early reconstruction of a historic garden, is famous for its six parterres of geometric splendour, its beautifully trained wall fruit and its rich borders. This garden is a spectacular example of The National Trust for Scotland's early awareness of the emerging discipline of garden history. When, in 1952, the Trust took over the care of Pitmedden, its lower walled enclosure was a well run working market garden, though its origins were much earlier. Pitmedden dates at least from the last quarter of the 17th century when Sir Alexander Seton, a member of an ancient family of Scottish landowners built a new house and garden on the site. The inscription 'FUNDAT 2 MAY 1675' carved into the lintel of the garden entrance has the initials of Alexander Seton and his wife Dame Margaret Lauder above.

Pimedden today is a most beautiful garden. The formal elements of the main parterre, the crisp box

◀▲ Views of Pitmedden: the lintel stone above the original garden entrance; a bed in the northwest part of the lower terrace; and part of the long border

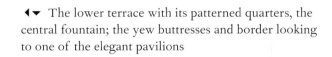
◀▾ The lower terrace with its patterned quarters, the central fountain; the yew buttresses and border looking to one of the elegant pavilions

patterning, and yew obelisks have matured, looking as well before they receive their summer bedding as when they are in full flower. On the high walls are exceptionally well-trained wall fruits. Borders lining two sides are rich and mature, and a small internal raised terrace to the south now allows for a viewing of the lower walled garden over a low crenellated beech hedge. This garden has developed a generous, well-proportioned formality that is the result of skilled gardening. The upper eastern terrace around the modest house has a rose garden and two, more recent, formal beds with pleasant avenues of pleached lime around them.

The late 17th century saw Scots making a creative contribution in terms of gardening, garden-making and plantsmanship that has continued to the present day. There were a number of Royal gardens, including those of Stirling Castle, Falkland Castle and Holyroodhouse, and there were other Seton family gardens. Alexander and his brother had been brought up by their kinsman, George, Lord Seton, who had made a great walled garden at Niddry Castle (where the author of the first Scots gardening book, John Reid, had been a gardener for short time). Sir William Bruce (1630–1710) who was Surveyor General for Charles II, and familiar with the work of Le Nôtre at Vaux le Vicomte and Versailles, completed the Palace of Holyroodhouse in Edinburgh as well as laying out formal gardens at Balcaskie and Kinross.

No records remain of the early garden at Pitmedden owing to a fire in 1818 that destroyed the family house and its contents. Few clues were left on the ground, though during the removal of the market garden it was found that there had been two burn-fed water outlets in the garden, one on the upper terrace where Sir Alexander had a fountain, and another in the lower parterre. Nothing revealing

the actual layout of the parterre was found, so at the suggestion of Dr James Richardson, a former Inspector of Ancient Monuments, the Trust used the bird's-eye view of Holyrood House in James Gordon of Rothiemay's 1647 view of Edinburgh, as a basis for the reconstruction of the great parterre garden. Three of the quarters take their inspiration from this picture, the symmetry of their square and rectangular beds and flourishes traced in box. The southeastern quarter centres on a sundial found at Pitmedden, thought to be contemporary with the original garden. Its long box beds spell out the words 'Tempus fugit'. The lion quarter in the northeast bed centres on a stone lion, one of two found at Pitmedden (the other was acquired by Drum Castle in 1989). The fourth quarter was designed by Dr Richardson as a tribute to Sir Alexander Seton, incorporating his coat of arms and the mottos SUSTENTO SANGUINE SIGNA (With blood I bear the stardard) and MERCES HAEC CERTA LABORUM (This sure reward of our labours). Flanking diagonally are the Scottish emblems: saltire and thistle.

The period geometry of the garden was

▲ Pitmedden in its market-garden days in 1948
▼ An early photograph *c.* 1906 by the sundial

Wall fruit, an old 'Worcester Pearmain' apple, and two red pear trees, 'Louise Bonne of Jersey', part of the fruit allée, *Achillea ptarmica* 'Boule de Neige'

Lady Mary's Pond, in
the woodland to the
south of the garden

combined with the 1950s passion for bedding plants, and the parterre shapes were densely planted to present a brilliant and lasting display for visitors. Each year the parterre has blazed with thousands of bright-coloured plants, demonstrating changes in public taste: at first, alyssum, begonias, wallflowers, antirrhinums, marigolds and ageratum dominated. Nowadays, although alyssum, begonias and marigolds are still used, the varieties are different and petunias, impatiens, grey-foliaged senecios and even a few perennials have been added to the palette. The Head Gardener, Susan Burgess, plants the parterre about mid-May from bedding raised in the greenhouses, using more plants than formerly

'to get dense blocks of colour and also to keep weed growth down'.

The other great feature of the mid-20th century, the mixed border, was also incorporated. Very fine borders run around the high garden walls, backed by the fan-trained and espaliered fruit trees. These are mostly apples with some pears. A few of the old Bramley apple trees on the east wall are about a century old. Neatly tiered up to the top of the wall, they are 6 metres or so in extent. Most of the wall fruit is younger: apple and pear cultivars put in at the time of the Trust's reconstruction of the garden. White currant, redcurrant and gooseberry bushes are trained trimly on the north-facing wall

The great stairway into the lower garden in past days when the vegetation was much higher, note the ivy over the far gatepost

above the raised platform. The borders contain inulas, rodgersias, geraniums and several kinds of thalictrum including the tall, fluffy, lilac-flowered *Thalictrum delavayi*, and *T. diffusiflorum* as well as the pink-purple *T. aquilegiifolium*.

The great terrace is centred on a fountain built in the 1950s from a mixure of Pitmedden stone and the carved stones that once formed part of the destroyed old Cross at Linlithgow in West Lothian, designed and built by Robert Mylne to commemorate the Restoration of Charles II, and taken down in 1805. The split pebble paving around the fountain was done in traditional form, with pebbles from the Dee, by Henry Macdonald, the then-estate mason. It is fed from a fountain and pool reconstructed on the upper terrace. This water also feeds a font set into the wall in a recess of the stair leading down to the great parterre. The whole garden is opened up along this east-west axis by means of a simple but effective innovation that entailed clearing and mowing a ride beyond the wrought-iron gate in the west wall, leading the eye to a substantial block of natural granite beyond. The intricacies of the fountains inside the walled garden, contrast dramatically with this rugged slab on the outside.

Half a century later, the parterre has become a period piece that demonstrates the aims and concerns of the Trust in the mid-20th century and an early practical application of garden history as it was appreciated at the time. The two parterre gardens, added in the upper terrace at the end of the 20th century, also took their inspiration from a painting by Gordon of Rothimay, in this case of the patterned garden for the George Heriot School. The south parterre is planted with herbs such as lavender, santolina and thyme, interspersed with coloured gravels, the north shows a patterned knot garden of coloured gravels. Both are consistent with the plants and ornamentation known to have featured in gardens of the 17th century, though not authentic reconstructions.

Large topiary buttresses of yew are spaced along the original west wall that separates the upper and lower terraces and provides height from which to view the geometries of the main parterre below. Between the buttresses are shrubs and climbers that benefit from the shelter and come into flower early, such as *Clematis armandii*, crinodendron, daphnes and honeysuckles, including the unusual orange-flowered *Lonicera ciliosa*. The elegant main stairway to the lower garden is set centrally within the wall. Two garden pavilions with elegant ogee roofs, contemporary with the original wall, provide endpieces of charm and style for the west wall.

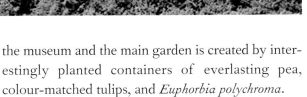

Adjacent to the house, through a courtyard of pleached hornbeam, is a Museum of Farming Life that contains an extensive historic collection of farm and gardening tools and domestic artefacts. Explanations as to how the 40-hectare estate was managed, draw on the collections and researches of Major James Keith. He was the last owner to farm here and it was he who ran the walled garden as a market garden. Attached to the museum is a small modern herb garden and apple alleé. A link between

the museum and the main garden is created by interestingly planted containers of everlasting pea, colour-matched tulips, and *Euphorbia polychroma*.

A woodland walk runs around the walled garden, along the waterway that flows into the Bronie Burn. Beyond is a lovely mixture of wild and naturalised plants, including butterbur, ramsons and pink purslane, beautiful trees and shrubs such as *Rubus spectabilis* with its raspberry-red flowers, the wildness, offsetting the neat perfection within the walls.

▲ The stairway which now has just a few small ferns growing on it.

▲ Clipping the box hedging

▼ Aerial view of all six of the geometric gardens, the sentinel yew on the left has been given the status of a Scottish Heritage tree.

Threave Garden

Threave House, near Castle Douglas in Dumfries and Galloway, has developed into a beautiful garden of considerable character. The National Trust for Scotland's gardener training school and demonstration garden has none of the condescension or bittiness characteristic of the genre; simply a presentation of good gardening. It is useful that the terrain is varied so that different habitats and garden styles can quite naturally be contained within its 28 hectares. Take a circuit of its spacious grounds and you can find woodland, a walled garden, orchard, borders, and rose, water heather and rock gardens

Threave is a substantial achievement on the part of the Trust which conceived and created the garden on an estate left to it in 1957 by Major Alan Gordon. In 1960, on the recommendation of the Trust's Gardens Committee, it was decided that Threave House would become a School for

◀◀ The planting in the borders softens the lines of the house

◀ Part of the large and well-planted rock garden

189

▶ The daffodil season always gives a wonderful show

▶▶ A Threave student at work weeding the strawberry bed in summer

Practical Gardening, and also act as a model of good gardening practice. The first Director, and the garden's shaping hand, Bill Hean, had for his raw materials, a half-hectare walled garden with a collection of old apple trees, a glasshouse and 28 hectares of land, some hilly, some boggy. A large daffodil collection, planted by the Major, and spectacular in spring, was naturalised on a bank to the northeast of the house.

Threave House, a large red sandstone building, built in the late 19th century by C.G.H. Kinnear for William Gordon, a Liverpool businessman, lies in a dell looking to the west. The garden is interestingly hilly, though the heavy loam soil has a tendency towards waterlogging in the heavy rainfall of this region. The first students at Threave completed their practical work actually making the garden. Nowadays, Threave takes students from universities or colleges who wish to do a year's practical work and to get a thorough grounding in gardening in what has become an important Trust garden, with an increasing flow of visitors. Graduates have gone on to influential posts not only in the Trust's own gardens but in others worldwide.

The mature trees and shrubs of the long entrance drive and landscaped car park make a good first impression, and fortunately the hilliness of Threave swallows crowds, so that you can enjoy a degree of privacy even when visitor numbers are high. My preferred starting point is the woodland garden, past the rose garden and not far down from the entrance which is also an information centre, shop and restaurant.

◀ Part of the walled kitchen garden with its apple trees, and vegetables

chaffinches are all around and sparrows and black-birds rustle among the leaves of the forest floor. The herbaceous plants include those familiar in the wider landscape, such as foxgloves, and there are a others that naturalise readily, such as tall bear's breeches *Acanthus spinosus*, martagon lilies *Lilium martagon* and other Turk's cap lilies These are accompanied by a glorious medley of woodland plants and shade-loving cultivars from all over the world such as the late flowering willow gentian *Gentiana asclepiadea*, campanulas, meconopsis, and many kinds of hosta and lily. A large bank of woodland primulas that has self-seeded and interbred provides a fantastic midsummer burst of bright colour that can stand comparison to the gaiety of the azaleas in spring.

Rock is not far from the surface in this garden, and the imposing rock garden now seems almost like a natural feature with a waterfall and pool at its base. Dwarf conifers and willows and small ever-green shrubs such as *Gaultheria* grow among the heathers and other flowers of the upper reaches. You see many distinctive cultivars around the

Wide paths lead through the woodland walk with banks of flowers and shrubs planted all though. There are native trees such as beech, oak and birch with mature exotics such as Douglas and silver firs, (*Pseudotsuga menziesii* and *Abies alba*) underplanted with smaller trees such as the paperbark maple *Acer griseum* and a number of azaleas and smaller rhodo-dendron cultivars that come into their own in early spring. The whole area is rich in bird life: song thrushes and warblers sing on the branches,

▲ Azaleas make a fine early summer display, the house visible between the conifers.

◀ Rhododendrons and eucalpytus with the information centre in the distance.

◥ There is a huge variety of primulas at Threave, blooming over a long period from spring into summer.

▶▶ Threave has a good range of dahlias and penstemons. Beyond this dahlia bed is the stables.

water, such as an orange *Trollius chinensis* 'Golden Queen' and a neat hybrid of the fishing rod dierama *Dierama pulcherrimum* called 'Miranda'.

Linger on your way to the walled garden to admire the exceptional long border down the outside of south wall. Mixed flowers and shrubs of all kinds include groups of trilliums, salvias and striking clumps of euphorbias. Great bursts of orange, gold and red day lilies blend beautifully with the tall yellow daisies of *Telekia speciosa*, an imposing plant not quite so large as elecampane *Inula hookeri*. A particular kind of *Inula royleana*, which has the characteristic bright yellow flower but with outer petals drooping downwards, was introduced by Magnus Ramsay from his expeditions to the western Himalayas. He also introduced the fragrant yellow *Morina coulteriana* to Threave.

The pleasant terrace where you can have tea amid the scent of sweet peas and honeysuckle while looking out over the garden.

Within the walled garden there are soft fruit and vegetable displays to gladden the heart, plentiful fruit trees and more flower borders. The garden does not do as many trials as it used to but provides a good place to see a selection of fruit and vegetable varieties. Raspberries do well in Scotland and two of the best are 'Malling Jewel' and 'Glen Prosen'. Of the blackcurrants, another Scottish speciality, 'Ben Sarek' was the first choice. Among the apples are good old favourites such as 'Ellison's Orange' and 'Fortune', and newer varieties such as 'Discovery' and 'Epicure'. Some apples are grown on small trees, others as cordons, and there are beautifully fan-trained pears. A fan-trained redcurrant on a north wall was an unusual idea for an ornamental and productive use for a difficult site.

The trend over the last decade has been to reduce use of pesticide where possible. Bob Brown, who has worked at Threave for nearly forty years regards the clay soil in this western part of the garden as quite good to work but fairly acid, but it can be successfully sweetened with magnesian limestone. The garden can get cold in winter, but Bob Brown noted that more losses were due to the winter wet than to frost.

The Victorian-style glasshouse in the walled garden was rebuilt in 1997 after a heavy snowfall demolished its predecessor. Modern materials and versatile temperature control make it possible to grow and overwinter tender and only partly hardy plants. Climbing plants such as the cascading yellow tropaeolum known as canary creeper *Tropaeolum peregrinum* are a special feature.

In the southeast part of the garden lie the arboretum, heather garden and orchard. On an early visit to Threave I was delighted to find that Bill Hean had an interest in Scottish varieties of pear and the beginnings of a collection that had come to Threave from Mylnefield in Invergowrie. The pears had all been collected from old orchards in the Carse of Gowrie. Some of these were relict monastic orchards and of considerable antiquity. Thanks to the prescient collecting, the fruit trees can still be grown and propagated so that present-day gardeners, who are once again interested in taste and the growing of regional varieties, can find a supply of authentic stock.

We now know that fruit-growing in Scotland was more widespread between the 17th and 19th centuries than had been supposed. Some of the pears were distinct Scottish varieties such as 'Charnock', and 'Grey Achen' (syn. 'Chaumontel'. Others have been grown in many parts of Britain for many centuries. Some may have come over with the Norman conquest, their names acquiring a Scottish inflection; 'Golden Knapp', which was grown by Edward I's fruiterers was known as "Goud Knap" in the early 19th century in Gowrie, and 'Cuisse Madame' became "Cush Madam".

Along with the arboretum and heather garden on the slopes above Threave House are plantings of holly and azalea and a woodland path. The daffodil collection has been augmented and the early spring extravaganza is at its best on the flower-covered slopes near the house. I prefer to leave the rose garden as a last pleasure. Laid out semi-formally on the slopes below the information centre, it contains a good selection of varieties, especially shrub and species roses.

The boarded terrace of the information centre restaurant extends partly into this garden and from here you can enjoy a view over the garden to the west and southwest, and the scents of the roses. There is a wealth of garden birds in this area and you are likely to be joined by a chaffinch or sparrow (the latter now uncommon in the south of the UK) eager for a crumb. There is also the opportunity to enjoy at close quarters the clematis, roses and honeysuckles that entwine the balustrade.

The woodland garden, one of the most attractive areas of Threave with woodland plants from all over the world

Other Gardens

The gardens that follow include properties that are owned by The National Trust for Scotland and under guardianship agreements, or leased to other organisations, or where the Trust has a strong association. At some properties there is a gardener, at others the property manager (in some cases with help from a contractor) cares for the garden.

At Alloa Tower and Dunkeld there were significant designed landscapes, of which very little now remains. Alloa Tower, which is believed to have had one of the most astonishing gardens in Scotland, is managed by the Trust. Stanley Hill at Dunkeld, a fragment of the designed landscape of Dunkeld House, laid out in 1730 by the Duke of Atholl, came to the Trust in 1954. Stanley Hill and the Banks of Tay and Braan are closely associated with another Trust property, The Hermitage.

In the case of Pollok House, Sir John Stirling Maxwell placed his 458-hectare estate under the protection of the first Conservation Agreement of the Trust, of which he was a founder member, and it is because of this connection that this property figures here. In 1966 Mrs Anne Maxwell gave the estate to the City of Glasgow. From 1998, the Trust was invited to manage the house in partnership with Glasgow City Council; the gardens and Country Park and Burrell Collection are managed and maintained by the City Council.

Dirleton Castle is owned by the Trust, but both castle and garden are managed by Historic Scotland. At properties such as J.M. Barrie's Birthplace, Souter Johnnie's Cottage and Weaver's Cottage, owned and cared for by the Trust, small gardens have been made to complement the properties in a way appropriate to their period, history and usage.

Alloa Tower

▲ Alloa Tower among the trees with the town behind it

This massive tower house on the north bank of the River Forth, dating from the 1300s and one of the oldest and largest still surviving, is understood to have once been the centre of a palatial complex with extensive gardens. The tower retains its original oak beams, vaulting and well; the domed Italianate staircase to the Great Hall was added in the 18th century by John Erskine the 6th Earl of Mar. The mansion adjoining the Tower was destroyed by fire in 1800. Of the once-great gardens, only plans and other documents,

and small fragments of the physical landscape, remain.

The 6th Earl consciously designed the gardens at Alloa as a symbol of Scotland's 18th-century status. Research by the architectural historian Margaret Stewart shows the scope and ambition of his plans and how much they were a fusion of the ideas of the great French gardens, especially Versailles, and Scottish heritage. His intention was to transform the historic tower with its associations with war and Erskine lineage, placing it in a complex of interactive elements that celebrated the

Scottish enlightenment, blending the aesthetics of high culture with a pride in Scottish industrialisation, peace and prosperity.

Though his high-profile political career dipped and ducked with the failure of the rebellion he led in 1715, his exile and loss of title, the Earl was always consistent in his creative desire for improvement of his ancestral lands, which were also the source of his great wealth. He encouraged the development of trade and industry from the coal, and built a deep-water harbour for the town on the Forth. In 1710 he opened the Gartmorn Dam north-east of Alloa, to drain the mines and power the town's mills. The improved waterworks also fed the pools south of his house, and ponds for fish and waterfowl. Defoe, passing through Alloa in 1722-24 on one of his Scottish tours, observed the thriving town and its busy port flourishing with local and international trade. The 6th Earl's interest in improvement and architecture continued. While he was in exile, in 1727, he sent architectural drawings for Alloa's improvement to his son Thomas.

Alloa Tower lies below the town, on the edge of the Forth flood plain. The Earl's landscape plan linked the Tower with the historic dependencies and with modern industrial enterprise. He created vistas to local landmarks such as Sauchie Tower, the water engine at the Heughs of Clackmannan, Clackmannan Tower, Old Stirling Bridge and Elphinstone House. Alloa Gardens were also linked by a series of avenues to Stirling Castle, itself an embodiment of Scottish pride, built at a moment of wealth and independence.

The Coalgate or Lime Tree Walk on the eastern boundary of the gardens, between the harbour and the town, was part of the designed landscape. It was laid out in 1706, hedged to protect the gardens from the noise and dust of the coal carts and lined with lime trees. A plan from 1710 details the grounds at Alloa covering four square miles, showing vegetable gardens, orchards, orangeries, wildernesses, parterres and bosquets. Defoe admiringly noted that the Earl had achieved 'every Thing that Nature and Art can do'.

By the end of the century it appears that the gardens had been changed considerably, as disclosed by a family portrait by David Allen that shows grounds with open parkland. Later development ate up the rest of the estate

The lime avenue that joins the adjacent housing development with the town, via the grounds of the Tower

and now only a ghostly contour of part of the 6th Earl's gardens are thought to be traceable.

Alloa Tower had been in the continuous possession of the Erskine family until 1988 when the 13th Earl of Mar and Kellie, joined with Clackmannan District Council to form what later became the Clackmannanshire Heritage Trust. They undertook an award-winning restoration that included the Lime Tree Walk as an important feature of the landscape of the town of Alloa. Alloa Tower is now managed by The National Trust for Scotland on behalf of the Clackmannanshire Heritage Trust, with funding from the Clackmannanshire Council. Much interesting work remains to be done in tracing the history and development of the designed landscape around the Tower.

Angus Folk Museum

▶ A cheese press in front of the Angus folk Museum

The Museum is housed in a row of cottages, and at the farm steading opposite where the larger agricultural items are displayed. The six 18th-century cottages contain the domestic section. Plants soften the line of the small cottages, built in the 1790s for Angus estate workers, and there is a small garden, the combination of perennials and climbers giving a homely appearance to the terrace. The collection of rural artifacts originally assembled by Jean, Lady Maitland is designed to give an insight into the lives of the rural workers and the changes over the last two centuries. The Museum was previously the responsibility of local trustees and passed to the care of the Trust in 1957 The steading building was donated by the Earl of Strathmore and Kingholme.

Balmerino Abbey

The ancient sweet chestnut *Castanea sativa* at Balmerino

A huge ancient Spanish chestnut *Castanea sativa*, one of the oldest in Scotland and believed to have been planted by Mary Queen of Scots in 1565 (and on the list of 100 Heritage Trees of Scotland) grows a little distance from the site of the Abbot's House, in the grounds of the ruined Cistercian monastery of Balmerino in north Fife, which was founded in 1229. An alternative story suggested that it was planted by Queen Ermengarde, the widow of William the Lion and mother of Alexander II, who invited the Cistercians of Melrose Abbey to build a daughter house on the Balmerino site. It was thought to be the place where St Merimac, a monk who accompanied St Rule when he brought back the bones of St Andrew to Scotland, landed. Queen Ermengarde was buried before the High Altar in 1233 but it was desecrated, and a wooden cross now marks her grave. It would be very unlikely for a sweet chestnut to live so long and the Trust's dating of the tree suggests a maximum of 500 years. In 1605 the the Abbey and its land were granted to Sir James Elphinstone, 1st Lord Balmerino. The ruins are not at the time of writing open to the public as they are being stabilised, but can be seen from the grounds. Balmerino Abbey was given to the Trust in 1936 by the Earl of Dundee.

J.M. Barrie's Birthplace

James Matthew Barrie, the writer and playwright was born in 1860 in a small stone-built cottage in Kirriemuir in Angus. He was the third son, and seventh surviving child, of Margaret Ogilvy and David Barrie, a handloom weaver. The inspiration for his best-known work, *Peter Pan*, seems likely to have sprung from his early years at Kirriemuir, where he attempted to console his mother for the death of his oldest brother, the child who would never grow up. Barrie himself said that the small wash-house at the back of the cottage was his first theatre. It is supposed that it was also the model for the 'Wendy House'.

Barrie's essays collected as *Auld Licht Idylls* published in 1888 (under a pseudonym), were a series of stories and sketches of his life in Kirriemuir (fictionalised as 'Thrums') written in a style that became known as the 'Kailyard School'. In 1902 he published *The Little White Bird* about his relationship with Sylvia Llewelyn Davies and her five sons. Ideas in this book were elaborated in *Peter Pan*, a play performed in London in 1904. In 1906 chapters from the first book were published as *Peter Pan in Kensington Gardens*; then, in 1911, a prose version of the play was published as *Peter and Wendy*.

When Barrie died in 1937, (he was buried, at his own request, in Kirriemuir) it was proposed that his house be moved to the USA; but it was purchased by Mr D. Alves and given to The National Trust for Scotland. In 1980 when the next door house came up for sale it was bought by the Trust and in 1999 its yard was made into a garden for Barrie's Birthplace, to a design by Robert Grant.

It is predominantly a children's garden with flower borders with an edging of ship's rope. There are plans for these borders to be replanted with cultivars with names associated with Barrie's best-known characters. There are *agapanthus* 'Peter Pan', 'Wendy' and 'Tinkerbell', for example, and a Michaelmas daisy 'Peter

Living willow crocodile

Pan', an iris 'Tinkerbell, hebe and nerine 'Smee'. In addition, there are a fuchsia, chrysanthemum, rose, clematis and many others named after Peter Pan, Wendy and Tinkerbell to chose from.

The old coal sheds in the garden are now a 'Pirates' Workshop' (or education room). A 5-metre long crocodile of living willow makes a interactive sculptural art form that will swallow child and adult alike. and wooden Peter Pan artefacts in the form of an oak cannon, a pirate's chest and several hogshead (whisky) barrels contribute to the garden scene.

Barry Mill

Orchard at Barrie Mill by Ken Bushe

There are records of a mill on this site since at least 1539, and Barry Mill was the last water-powered mill to work in Angus, producing oatmeal into the 1970s and animal feed until 1982, when damage to the mill lade (the watercourse that diverts water to the mill) led to its closure. The Trust bought the buildings in 1988 and gradually a process of restoration took place. As well as milling demonstrations, the property has attractive grounds of nearly a hectare, including a delightful small orchard with Scottish apple cultivars. The Property Manager has the help of a sheep in his grass management. There is also some woodland and a waymarked walk. Among the garden plants is a collection of helianthemums (the small floriferous shrubs, also known as rock roses or sun roses) of the 'Ben' series which includes the well-known 'Ben Nevis' with its orange, crimson-centred flowers, and the carmine-red 'Ben Hope'. This group was bred in Monifieth near Dundee by a Scottish jute merchant called John Nicoll who died in 1926. He raised 17 helianthemums, of which 14 are still extant. The remaining 3 are on the NCCPG Pink Sheet of sought-after plants which it is hoped will be found – perhaps in a corner of some garden – and kept in cultivation.

Canna House

Coroghon House (now the bothy) and its garden were built by Hector MacNiell on the small island of Canna in the Inner Hebrides in the late 18th century. In the 1860s, his grandson, Donald MacNiell built the present Canna House in the centre of the walled garden, and took the upper story off Coroghon House. The garden of about a hectare was laid out in compartments and terraces. A path leads from a central gate through an escallonia tunnel to the front of the house. A drive also leads to the front of the house from a side gate. The walled garden is now mainly disused and overgrown but has considerable charm, and the main elements and compartments, divided by fuchsia hedges, are still recognisable. There are many fine plants, including a massive olearia.

As well as the escallonia tunnel, this island garden, frozen in time, has historic features such as a drive flanked by herbaceous and shrub borders, a vegetable garden, a Vine House, a long herbaceous border on the top terrace and black pebble paths with ceramic rope-tile edges. There is also a croquet lawn, a drying lawn and hawthorn and fuchsia hedges. The orchard has a

Gardener at Canna
House

remarkable collection of rare fruit trees, and there are espalier fruits against the walls and a nursery area. Ornamental shrubs and trees, roses, lawns and wild grassland also feature. Dr John Lorne Campbell,who previously owned the house, was a collector of moths, and his butterfly and moths garden survives. Almost all the features of the built environment remain: ornamental iron gates, benches and seats, small rockeries, engine houses, and utility and storage houses. The garden is surrounded by a woodland with walks and vistas, benches, a hen range and summer house.

Dr Campbell and his wife Margeret Fay Shaw bought Canna in 1938 and gifted it (together with the adjacent island of Sanday) to the The National Trust for Scotland in 1981. Dr Campbell had established himself as one of the 20th century's leading Gaelic scholars and included his library in the gift to ensure a future for Gaelic study on Canna. From Canna House there are splendid views across Canna Harbour to the Isle of Sanday. The Trust intends to restore the garden in the near future, to ensure that it will once again provide a perfect setting for the house and preserve the vision of the Campbells.

Dirleton Castle in its
pleasant grounds

Dirleton Castle

Dirleton Castle in East Lothian, built by John de Vaux in the 13th century on the site of an earlier castle, had changed hands between the Scots and the English repeatedly before Robert the Bruce ordered it to be partly demolished to prevent it falling into English hands again. It held a commanding position on a rocky outcrop and was subsequently ruined and rebuilt several times. The Halyburtons, who owned it from the late 14th century, made a magnificent residence of Dirleton. During the 16th century the then-owners, the Ruthven family, extended the castle and made terraced gardens to the west of its walls, adding a walled garden and the oddly-shaped beehive doocot. It is possible that the sunken bowling green was structured on one of these parterres.

Now owned by The National Trust for Scotland, and managed under the guardianship of Historic Scotland, the ruined but still handsome castle is no longer surrounded by bog and marsh or its freshwater ditch but by an enjoyable restored Arts and Crafts garden with a continuous herbaceous border reckoned to be one of the longest in Britain. This garden, made in the 1920s, was converted from a 19th-century renovation which saw the introduction of new geometric parterres by the Nisbets who owned the castle from 1663. They later moved to live at Archerfield House, about a mile distant, though they continued to use Dirleton as their garden.

Dunkeld, Stanley Hill

Stanley Hill is possibly the hillock or *dun* from which Dunkeld took its name. On the banks of the River Tay, this small town, characterised by Queen Victoria as 'the beginning of the Highlands', held a strategic position on the pass between Birnam Hill and the Newtyle Hills on either side of the Tay — at 'the gates of the mountains'. This gateway between Highlands and Lowlands, has been an important site from earliest times, with Pictish, and possibly Neolithic, settlements established there which were the sites of much violence. The little town of Dunkeld was totally destroyed in 1689 in the Battle of Dunkeld. The town was built back to the east (the Duke of Atholl, being determined to retain his view of the Cathedral) and thrived for a while, but declined after the building of the Tay Bridge and the coming of the railway to the southern bank of the river. The Trust was given twenty small houses in Cathedral and Cross Street in the old part of Dunkeld (not open to the public) which, in collaboration with Perth and Kinross Council, it has restored and let.

Stanley Hill as it now is represents the designed landscape built about 1730 by the Duke of Atholl for Dunkeld House which is thought to have been situated to the west. The Duke heightened the original mound and gave it a fortified appearance emulating the German landscape style, adding cannons. The icehouse, built into the mound by the Duke, and reached by steps, is still in existence. Stanley Hill is owned by the National Trust for Scotland and maintained by Perth and Kinross Council.

There are many fine trees on the estate, including the Dunkeld larches, among which were some of the earliest specimens of the European larch *Larix decidua* to have been planted in Scotland by the 2nd Duke of Atholl in 1738. Japanese larches *Larix kaempferi* were planted here by the 7th Duke and became a successful forestry species. These trees eleven of which survive, were the parents of the first hybrid larches, noted in 1904. One of the tallest trees in Britain, a Douglas fir of 59 metres, grows close by the banks of the Braan in Craigvinean Forest above another Trust property, the Hermitage.

▼ The small kitchen garden in the making at Holmwood

Holmwood House

Holmwood House, in the district of Cathcart to the south of Glasgow, is the crowning achievement of Alexander Thomson who designed many fine houses and Glasgow institutions in the mid-19th century. He was known as 'Greek Thomson' because his chosen style reflected the symmetry and classic lines of the ancients, though the epithet could just as well have been 'Egyptian' in view of his other main thematic motif.

Thomson built Holmwood, his most elaborate country house villa, in the years 1857–58, for Robert Couper, a Glasgow businessman who wished to have a fine house close to his papermill. More than any of his other designs, Holmwood signals Thomson's success as an architect and reflects his skills, especially in relation to

▶ An engraving of
Holmwood c. 1868

decoration and proportion. It is large, elegant and asymmetrical, with porticos and a cupola.

Thomson was also responsible for the interior detail including the plasterwork, joinery and floor tiling. The walls were painted with palms, fans or acanthus patterns and with scenes from the ancient world. The main windows of the first-floor drawing room, with their decorated woodwork, look out over a park with fine trees on a lawn that slopes away. The parkland and the views northward to the city and the country beyond, (and southwest to the neighbouring house, Sunnyside, a Gothic villa belonging to Robert's brother which was demolished in 1960s) were all taken into account in the design, but there is no evidence that Thomson had a part in the landscaping of the park. The kitchen garden does appear on his plans, however, though clearly as a working area. Referred to by Thomson as the 'inclosed kitchen garden', it is overlooked only by the service rooms of the villa. Thomson did make a sweeping drive that obliquely approaches the house. Although Glasgow has grown up all around since the house was built, so have the parkland trees and it is still possible to think oneself in the countryside.

The extraordinary house and its policies came to the Trust in 1997 in poor condition. House restoration of this complexity was time-consuming, but after the con-

tractors had moved off-site, progress was possible on the kitchen garden. From map evidence, supported by garden archaeology, what emerged was a picture of a garden on two levels, thought to extend to just under a hectare, with a glasshouse set against one of the corners, the foundations of which are still visible. A plan for re-instating a kitchen garden was developed and, following the employment of the part-time gardener, it has been possible to bring back Victorian fruit and flowers to this space. Once again there are vegetables such as leeks, potatoes (grown on rotation on small plots) and rhubarb crops at Holmwood, though on a modest scale. More fruit bushes are to be planted and the garden is gradually being brought back into fuller production.

Kittochside

The Museum of Scottish Country Life at Kittochside in East Kilbride, to the south of Glasgow, was created in partnership by The National Trust for Scotland and National Museums of Scotland. The Trust owns the farmland, the handsome Georgian farmhouse, its contents, and outbuildings, given by Mrs M.S.C. Reid in 1992. Ten generations of her family had prospered there since the 16th century. The National Museums brought to Kittochside the National Country Life Collection which shows how farming was carried out in the 1950s.

The Trust manages the farm's flower and vegetable gardens in keeping with the 1950s context of the property. In front of the house is an open lawn, rose beds and views south across the landscape. There are mature trees

and a good display of early spring snowdrops. A clipped shrubbery lies to the northeast, and the vegetable garden to the southwest is approached through a small woodland, full of naturalised daffodils and Spanish bluebells. A hawthorn hedge and box-lined paths mark out the beds, which the part-time gardener is steadily bringing back into full cultivation. A double herbaceous border draws the eye to the very fine sycamore which shades and shelters the garden beneath.

The surrounding meadows were always grazed, and the fields and lanes, never having been subjected to intensive pesticide spraying, retain wild flowers such as orchids, violas, meadowsweet, harebells (Scotch bluebells) and dog roses.

Mar Lodge

The vast estate at Mar Lodge, over 29,380 hectares in the Cairngorms National Park, is internationally important for its plant and animal life. The present Lodge, located five miles west of Braemar, was built in 1895–6 for the Duke and Duchess of Fife, and extensive flower gardens were laid out around it. The foundation stone of the Lodge was laid by Queen Victoria, who was grandmother to the duchess. In contrast to the Scottish Baronial style of building fashionable at the time, Mar Lodge aimed to be a woodland lodge (rather a grand one). Timber from the estate was used in its construction, and hunting trophies constituted its principal decoration. The Mar Estate was bought by The National Trust for Scotland in 1995, and they embarked on a long-term research and conservation project. The Lodge and the Ballroom are open to the public only on specified days but the wider estate is open all year.

The Lodge stands in a one of the most important wilderness areas in Europe. It is a landscape that has been managed over centuries; for timber and summer grazing grounds, for hunting, and now for nature conservation. The Mar Lodge Estate has a diversity of habitat that ranges from the valley floor to mountaintop. There is internationally significant alpine and wetland habitat, moorland, blanket bog and Caledonian pine forest with red squirrel, black grouse and capercaillie. It has significant Mesolithic archaeology in the form of worked flint and quartz, discovered and recognised during routine work on paths carried out by the Trust. There are archaeological remains from mediaeval and post-medieval times, and ruinous and derelict settlements that signal fluctuations in population and land use in this part of Scotland.

The Lodge, and its associated buildings in their various settings, reflect the considerable changes in land use, management and social values that occurred over the last century. The immediate landscape of the Lodge consisted of grand gardens and terraces. Photographs of the Lodge garden at the turn of the 20th century show fruit gardens and patterned beds brimming with flowers and several beds with splendid Russell lupins. Little now

remains, except for a partly walled area of just over a hectare of rough grass with a few trees, very quiet in comparison with the floristic superabundance of its past, but perhaps less incongruous within this magnificent wild setting.

One wall of a summerhouse still survives (in storage) and there are some lilacs and a few other trees. There are no plans at present for a fullscale restoration of this garden though the sundial is due for reinstatement, and a lupin border along the fence line has been suggested. Another interesting idea under discussion is for the re-creation of the patterns of the former beds and pathways by means of differential mowing to evoke the garden of the past in our imagination.

The gardens at Mar Lodge c. 1900

Pollok House

This grand country house is situated above White Cart Water in the 458-hectare grounds of the Pollok Estate. Pollok Park itself extends to 146 hectares. Pollok House, a Palladian mansion built for John Maxwell, was begun in 1747 by William Adam and finished under the direction of his son, John. It was built on a site slightly west of the former castle, the fourth house to have been built at Pollok, and the home of the Maxwells of Pollok for seven centuries.

Sir John Stirling Maxwell, a founder member of The National Trust for Scotland, made sympathetic enlargements from 1890 onwards in the form of single-storey extensions to the east and west, adding two garden pavilions of great charm in 1903. In the 1940s two huge stone lions by Hew Lorimer were made for the river entrance to the garden and he also provided a carved urn for the library parterre, leading from the eastern extension.

John Stirling Maxwell placed the whole estate under the protection of the first Conservation Agreement of the National Trust for Scotland. Mrs Anne Maxwell Macdonald gave the house and its collections of paintings, furniture and ceramics, to the City of Glasgow in 1966. The Trust was invited to manage the house in partnership with Glasgow City Council from 1998. The gardens, park and the Burrell Collection – also situated within Pollok Park – continue to be managed and maintained by the City Council.

The woodlands and walled garden date from 1741. In John Stirling Maxwell's time there was a substantial formal garden lying to the south, looking down to the river and framing the house. The shape of the garden and the terrace walls remain, but are at present, quite plain, mainly grass with a few beds and shrubs. Incongruously, a green hellebore *Helleborus viridis* grows from one of the terrace walls. A small formal garden has recently been made in the library parterre. Above it, a ride with shrub borders leads the eye up the hill. The woodland path adjacent leads up the hill to the 18th-century woodland garden with its magnificent trees, and the mound of an earlier castle. The wider estate is open to the public with paths to the mill and riverside and the Burrell Collection.

▶ One of Hew Lorimer's great lions

▶▶ Pollok House with a green hellebore growing from the wall

Souter Johnnie's Cottage

John Davidson was the village souter (shoemaker) in Kirkoswald in South Ayrshire. He was immortalised as *Souter Johnnie* by Robert Burns in 'Tam o' Shanter'. His small thatched cottage was been refurbished and furnished with period items, Burns memorabilia and a reconstructed souter's workshop. The little cottage garden contains a restored ale house with life-sized stone figures of the souter, the innkeeper and his wife.

Unst and Yell Estate

Unst, the most northerly inhabited island in Britain, is known locally as Rock Isle. It has a wild, lonely beauty with open beaches and cliffs, voes (inlets) and gentle hills, and even a small wood of sycamores. This last lies within the Trust's property at Halligarth, surrounded by monumentally high walls to the south of Halligarth House. The island as a whole is famous for its birds and plants, geology and archaeology, and it may, in the future, have some fame for its gardens, if it is feasible to research them and bring them sensitively back into use.

Among the members of the Saxby family (relatives of the donor of the estate, Miss Joy Sandison) were the naturalist Lawrence, Thomas, who was a botanist, and brother-in-law Henry, who wrote *The Birds of Shetland*. Halligarth House is close to Baltasound which is the largest settlement on Unst. The house is part 18th-century with a grander 19th-century part in front of it. The attractive, large and once-productive garden has a pattern of walls that suggests more than one enclosure. There are marvellous views and the adjacent Halligarth Wood is especially noted for its birds and plant life. The family burial ground, which is also walled, is reached by a beautiful pathway through the wood.

Old House of Lund, built in the 18th century for a merchant called John Ross, and ruinous at the time of writing, is on the west coast of the island, towards the southern end. It has a large garden with magnificent walls. The combination of the gaunt laird's house, the farm buildings and townships, the roofless kirk of St Olaf and its kirkyard, all in a landscape of great natural beauty and splendour, combine to make an unforgettable impression.

Weaver's Cottage

The cottage at Kilbarchan, in Renfrewshire, built in 1723 is typical of those occupied by weavers in the village which in the 1830s had about 800 working handlooms. It gives a glimpse into how the famous Paisley weavers lived and worked. The cottage is furnished with 19th-century furniture and period items, and the handloom in the basement continues to be worked to produce traditional fabrics. Some of the plants used to make natural dyes, such as woad and madder, are grown in the small, attractive cottage garden. There is a recessed space for bee boles in the garden wall. A bleaching green and washing line have been set out at the rear of the property. Scattered through the garden are historical artefacts, including an old cheese press and some curling stones, contributing to a sense of what village life would have been like in the past.

209

Gardeners are usually undersung. Those who were caring for the gardens while I was researching this book were themselves an inspiration and, while the whole book is in a way a tribute to them, this album page gives the Head Gardeners a personal credit. The gardens of The National Trust for Scotland require special skills, since the gardeners (and in some cases, property managers who are also Head Gardeners) need to know and respect the history of their property. They also have to deal with continuous growth and change, to develop the garden within its historic framework and to make sure there is plenty for the eager public to see and appreciate. They then have to get on with the business of practical gardening, knowing the soil, climate and responsiveness of their piece of land. It is owing to the people pictured on this page, their staff and volunteers that the gardens look as beautiful as they do.

1		3		4	5	6	7		8	
	2									
9		11								
	10			12	13	14	15		16	17
18		20	21							
	19			22	23	24	25	26	27	
28		30		31						
	29									
32	33	34		35	36		37	38		39

1 John Anderson, Inverewe
2 Sinclair Williamson, Kellie Castle
3 Peter Christopher, Hilll of Tarvit
4 Steve McNamara, Branklyn
5 Jim May, Greenbank
6 Susan Burgess, Pitmedden Garden
7 Volunteers at Newhailes
8 Nigel Price, Brodick and Crarae
9 Piers de Salis, Newhailes
10 Ann Steele, Regional Adviser, West
11 Susan Russell, Culzean
12 Philip Deacon, Malleny Garden
13 David Wheeler, Brodie Castle
14 Russell Shanks, House of Dun
15 Sinclair Williamson and other staff, Kellie Castle
16 Joanna Gough, Geilston
17 Kevin Wright, Fyvie Castle
18 Callum Pirnie, Crathes
19 Damon Powell, Castle Fraser
20 Mark Jeffery, Culross
21 Keith Blundell, Haddo House
22 Norman Tait, Harmony Garden

23 Robert Grant, Regional Adviser, Northeast
24 Melissa Simpson, Regional Adviser, South
25 Paul Chandler, Newhailes
26 Jan Haenraets, Head of Gardens
27 Andrew Leitch, Priorwood Garden
28 Diana Robertson, Drum Castle
29 Gavin Smith The Hill House
30 Andrew McCarron, Falkland Palace
31 Jim May, Greenbank
32 David Perry, The Pineapple
33 Veronica Barrington Gardens Administrator
34 Maurice Wilkinson, Arduaine and Crarae
35 Bob Brown, Threave Garden
36 Steven Kellett, Leith Hall
37 Nick Hoskins, Broughton House
38 Peter Christopher, Hill of Tarvit and Paul Chandler, Newhailes, and others
39 Clare Reaney, Inveresk Lodge Garden

Plant Collections in Gardens of The National Trust for Scotland

Cassiope stelleriana

Plant Collections in Gardens of The National Trust for Scotland:

ARDUAINE	Building up collection of *Rhododendron* (*Maddenia* subsection)
BARRY MILL	*Helianthemum* ('Ben' Series)
BRANKLYN	*Cassiope**Lilium* (developing collection of Asiatic lilies)
BRODICK	*Rhododendron** (*Maddenia* and *Falconera* subsections)
BRODIE	*Narcissus** (Brodie cultivars)
CRARAE	*Nothofagus**
CRATHES	*Dianthus**(Malmaisons)*Deutzia**Philadelphus*
DRUM	*Rosa pimpinellifolia* (developing collection of Scottish roses)
GREENBANK	*Bergenia**
INVERESK	*Tropaeolum**
INVEREWE	*Brachyglottis**Olearia**Rhododendron**(subsections *Maculifera, Glischra, Barbata*)
MALLENY	*Rosa** (19th-century shrub roses)

* denotes registered NCCPG Collection

Selected Plant Collections, species and cultivars as known:

Cassiope collection at BRANKLYN
'Askival', 'Askival Arctic Fox', 'Askival Snowbird', 'Askival Stormbird', 'Badenoch', 'Bearsden', 'Edinburgh', *C. fastigiata*, Freebird Group, 'Kathleen Dryden', *C. lycopodiodes*, *C. lycopodiodes* 'Beatrice Lilley', *C. lycopodiodes* 'Jim Lever', *C. lycopodiodes* 'Rokujo', 'Medusa', *C. mertensiana*, *C. mertensiana* var. *gracilis*, 'Randle Cooke', *C. selaginoides*, Snow-wreath group, *C. stelleriana*, *C. tetragona*, *C. wardii*, *C. wardii* 'George Taylor'.

Nothofagus species at CRARAE (12):
Nothofagus antarctica, *N. betuloides*, *N. cunninghamii*, *N. dombeyi*, *N. fusca*, *N. glauca*, *N. menziesii*, *N. nervosa*, *N. obliqua*, *N. pumilio*, *N. solanderi* var. *cliffortioides*, *N. solanderi* var. *solanderi*

Tropaeolum collection at INVERESK:
T. azureum, *T. beuthii*, *T. brachyceras*, *T. ciliatum* subsp. *septentrionale*, *T. hookerianum* subsp. *austropupureum*, *T. hookerianum* subsp. *hookerianum*, *T. hookerianum*. subsp. *pilosum*, *T. incisum*, *T. moritzianum*, *T. pentaphyllum*, *T. polyphyllum*, *T. sessilifolium*, *T. speciosum*, *T. tenuirostre*, *T. tricolor*, *T. tuberosum* var. *lineamaculatum* 'Ken Aslet'

Brodie daffodil 'Daviot'

Apple 'Worcester Pearmain'

▲ Brodie daffodil 'Kinforth Brodie'

National Plant Collection of 19th-century Shrub Roses at MALLENY:

'Céleste' c. 1797-; 'Chloris' 1835-; 'Königin von Dänemark' 1826-; 'Félicité Parmentier' 1834; 'Madame Legras de Saint Germain' 1846-; 'Madame Plantier' 1835; 'Bourbon Queen' 1834; 'Malton' 1830; 'Kronprinzessin Viktoria' 1888; 'Louise Odier' 1851; 'Madame Ernest Calvat' 1888; 'Madame Isaac Pereire' 1880; 'Souvenir de la Malmaison' 1843; 'Zéphirine Drouhin' 1868; 'Blairii Number Two' 1845; 'Amadis' 1829; 'Morletii' 1883; 'Blanchefleur' 1835; 'Fantin-Latour' 1900-; 'William Lobb' 1855; 'Fellemberg' 1835-; 'Ards Rover' 1898; 'Isaphan' 1832-; 'La Ville de Bruxelles' 1836; 'Madame Zöetmans' 1830; 'Madame Hardy' 1832; 'De Rescht' 1880; 'Madame Knorr' 1855; 'Madame Delaroche-Lambert' 1851; 'Salet' 1854; 'Belle de Crécy' 1829; 'Cardinal de Richelieu' 1840; 'Duchesse d'Angoulême' 1821; 'Duchesse de Montebello' 1829-; 'Gloire de France' 1828; 'Président de Sèze' 1828; 'Tuscany Superb' 1837; 'Baronne Prévost' 1842; 'Mrs John Laing' 1887; 'Reine des Violettes' 1860; 'Stanwell Perpetual' 1838; 'Janet's Pride' 1892; 'Gloire des Mousseuses' 1852; 'Jeanne de Montfort' 1851; 'Louis Gimard' 1877; 'Nuits de Young' c. 1845; 'Alister Stella Gray'

1894; 'Madame Alfred Carrière' 1879; 'Rêve d'Or' 1869; 'William Allen Richardson' 1878; 'Spinosissima Grandiflora' 1818; 'Aimée Vibert' 1828; 'Baltimore Belle' 1843; 'Félicité Perpétue' 1827; 'The Garland' 1835; 'Narrow Water' 1883; 'Russelliana' 1840-; 'Spectabilis' 1833-; 'Belle Poitevine' 1894; 'Fimbriata' 1891; sericea subsp. Omeiensis f. pteracantha 1890; 'Duponti' 1817-; 'Gloire de Dijon' 1853; x harisonii 'Williams's Double Yellow' c. 1828; x harisonii 'Harrison's Yellow' 1830-.

The Scottish apple varieties grown in Scotland, planned for FYVIE:

'Alderman', 'Beauty of Moray', 'Bloody Ploughman', 'Braddick Nonpareil', 'Cambusnethan Pippin', 'Cardross Green', 'Clydesdale', 'Coul Blush', 'Cutler Grieve' 'Early Julyan', 'East Lothian Pippin', 'Galloway Pippin', 'Gogar Pippin', 'Green Kilpandy Pippin', 'Hawthornden', 'Hill's Seedling', 'Hood's Supreme', 'James Grieve', 'Lady of the Lake', 'Lady of the Wemyss', 'Lass o' Gowrie', 'Lemon Queen', 'Liddel's Seedling', 'Lord Rosebery', 'Lovacka Reneta', 'Love Beauty', 'Maggie Sinclair', 'Melrose', 'Pine Golden Pippin', 'Port Allen Russet', 'Red

▶ *Ourisia* 'Loch Ewe'

▶▶ *T. tuberosum* var. *lineamaculatum* 'Ken Aslett'

▶▶ Brodie daffodil 'Cotterton'

Sudeley', 'Rock', 'Scotch Bridget', 'Scotch Dumpling', 'Seaton House', 'Stark's Late Delicious', 'Stirling Castle', 'Stobo Castle', 'Tower of Glamis', 'Warden', 'Weight', 'Melrose', 'White Paradise', 'Yorkshire Aromatic'

Cultivars, not commercially available but possibly still growing in private collections:
'Annat Scarlet', 'Balgone Pippin', 'Bow Hill Pippin', 'Burntisland Spice', 'Burknott', 'Carberry Pippin', 'Clydesdale', 'Clyde Transparent', 'Contin Reinette', 'Court of Wick', 'Dalmahoy Pippin', 'Dalzell Pippin', 'Dumbarton Pippin', 'Edinburgh Cluster', 'Fair Maid of Perth', 'Fife Golden Pippin', 'Forfar Pippin', 'Gourdiehill No 9', 'Grey Leadington', 'James Welsh', 'Jenny Sinclair', 'Jolly Beggar', 'Keen's Seedling', 'Kerkan', 'Kinellan', 'Kinfauns Pippin', 'Kirton', 'Lady Kinloch', 'Luffness Castle', 'Luffness Matchless', 'Maiden', 'Malcolm's Delight', 'McGregor's Seedling', 'MacDonald's Scot', 'Moncrieffe', 'Muirfield',

'Naked Apple', 'Nancy King', 'Pencaitland Pippin', 'Pursemouth', 'Ravelston Pippin', 'Scarlet Golden Pippin', 'Scotchman', 'Scottish Chief', 'Summer', 'Sweet Topaz', 'Tankard', 'Tarvey Codlin', Teuchat Egg', 'Transparent', 'White Virgin' and 'White Wine'.

Index and Glossary

Abercummie, William, 67

Aberdeen, 3rd Marquess of, 98

Aberdeen, 4th Earl of, (Prime Minister 1852-1855), 98

Aberdeen, June, Marchioness of Aberdeen and Temair 98

Aberdeenshire Castles (in full, *The Castellated Architecture of Aberdeenshire*, 1849), 40, 99

Abies alba silver fir, 139

Abies grandis giant fir, *45*

Abies koreana Korean pine, 45

Abies spectabilis var. *brevifolia*, 56

Abutilon, 68

Abutilon 'Savitzii', *94*

Abutilon pictum 'Thompsonii', *94*

Acacia, 16

Acer cappadocium 'Aureum', 55, *132*

Acer griseum paperbark maple, 31

Acer palmatum Dissectum Atropurpureum Group, 13

Acer palmatum var. *rubrum*

Acer tataricum subsp. *ginnala* Amur maple, *55*

Achillea filipendula 'Goldplate', *185*

Achillea filipendula, *79*

Achillea ptarmica 'Boule de Neige', *180*

Achillea, 122

Acidanthera, 66

Aciphylla, 156

Adam, Robert (1728-92), Architect, principal exponent of neo-classical style in Britain, works include Culzean Castle and Charlotte Square, 63, 64, 69

Adam, William (1689-1748), Leading architect of the Scottish Enlightenment; work included Haddo House and House of Dun, 97, 98, 119, 120, 208

Adiantum, 159

Agapanthus, 122, 143, *143*

Ageratum, 98, 181

Akebia quinata, 135

Alchemilla, 65, 167

Alder, 175

Algae, 128

Alkanet *Pentaglottis sempervirens*, 128

Allason, Robert, 93

Allium caeruleum, 144

Allium cristophii, *185*

Alloa Tower, 196-199, *198*

Alloa, xi

Alpine strawberry 'Baron Solemacher', 103

Alstromeria, 116

Alves, Mr D, 201

Alyssum, *92*, 181

Amaranthus, 122

Amelanchier canadense, 94

Anaphalis triplinervis, 103

Anchusa capensis 'Blue Angel', 55

Anderson, John, Head Gardener, Inverewe, 138, 210-11

Anemone hupehensis Japanese anemone, 27

Anemone, 27, 86

Anemone, Japanese, 29, 115

Anemone, wood *Anemone nemorosa*, 41, 157, *170*

Anemonella thalictroides, 29

Angus Folk Museum, 200

Anthemis tinctoria, 153

Antirrhinum, 181

'Apothecary's Rose' *Rosa gallica* var. *officianalis*, 151

Apple, 65, 83, 103, 122, 147,185, *191*, 202

Apple: 'Bramley', 18; 'Charnock', 194; 'Court Pendu Plat', 185; 'd'Api', 185; 'Discovery', 194; 'Ellison's Orange', 194; 'Epicure', 194 : 'Galloway Pippin', 65; 'Grey Achen' (syn. 'Chaumontael'), 194; 'Lady of Wemyss', 65; 'Laxton's Fortune', 194; 'Melrose', 185; 'Seaton House', 65; 'Stirling Castle', 65; 'Thorle Pippin', 122: 'Worcester Pearmain', *180*; "Cush Madam" ('Cuisse Madame'), 195; "Goud Knap" ('Golden Knapp') 194

Apples, espalier, 60

Apricot, 102

Aralia elata, 131

Archerfield House, 204

Arduaine Garden, xiv, 1-5

Artemisia, 167

Ash trees, 120, 123

Asiatic hybrid lilies, 11

Asknish, 1

Asparagus pea, 61

Asparagus, 61, 88

Astilbe, 111

Astilbes, 69, 86, 142

Atholl, Duke of, 205

Athyrium filix-femina Lady fern, 159

Athyrium nipponicum var. *pictum*, 156

Auld Licht Idylls by J.M. Barrie, 201

Avens Dryas, 142

Avenue, 34, 86, 119

Awe, Loch, 44

Azaleas, *45*, 57, 192, 195

Azorella trifurcata, 156

Balcaskie, 179

Balfour, 19, 44

Balmerino Abbey, 200

Baltasound, 209

Bamboo, 156. 159

Banana *Musa basjoo*, 68

Barbata subsp. of *Rhododendron*, 139

Barmkin, outer defensive walling, *39*, 40

Barrie, J.M., birthplace, 197

Barrington, Veronica, Gardens Administrator, 210-211

Barry Mill, 202

Bartizan, small turret projecting from a corner of a castle or house, xiii, 21, 82,

Bauchop, Robert, *171*, 173

Bavarian Summer House, 16

Bavelaw Burn, Malleny, 163

Baxter, John, 98

Beckford, William, 19

Bee skep, 91, *148*

Beet, 103

Begonia, 65, 121, 167, 181

Bel, master masons of Aberdeen, 50

Bellflowers *Campanula*, 97, 111

Berberis, 164

Berberis thunbergii 'Aurea', 53

Bergenia, 94

Betula albosinensis var. *septentrionalis*, birch, 12

Birch *Betula*, *110*, 186

Birch *Betula pendula* 'Laciniata', 111

Birches, naturalised, *47*

Black Hamburg grapevine (correctly 'Schiava Grossa'), 167

Blackbird, 148

Blackie, Anna, 111

Blackie, Walter, 109-11, *110*

Bleaching green, 209

Blomfield, Reginald, 19

Bluebell, 37, 41, *45*, *47*, 68, 89, *101*, *110*, 128

Blundell, Keith, Head Gardener, Haddo House, 98, 210-211

Blyth, W.P., 93

Bogbean *Menyanthes trifoliata*, 4

Boonery, Culzean, 67

Borage, *Borago officianalis*, 163

Boscawen, J.P.T., 19

Boswell, James, 171

Bowles golden grass *Milium effusum* 'Aureum', 53

Bowling green, 41, 172

Box blights generic name for disease that spreads in damp conditions, involving two fungi, *Volutella* and *Cylindrocladium buxicola*, the latter present in Britain only since the 1980s, 88

Braan, River, xiv, *105*, *106*, 106, 197, 205

Brachyglottis brunonis Tasmanian grounsel tree, 139

Bradford, University of, 72

Branklyn Garden, xv, 7-13

Broad bean, purple, *149*

Brodick Castle, 14-19

Brodie Castle, 20-5, 95

Brodie daffodils, *21*, 95

Brodie House, 23

Brodie, Alexander Brodie of, 19th laird, 22

ACKNOWLEDGEMENTS

Thanks to all at The National Trust for Scotland, especially Isla Robertson, the Photo Librarian at Photographic Library, whose help with photography and archive material, and whose staunch support, were invaluable. Thanks also to Peter Burman, Director of Conservation at the Trust, who promoted the idea of this book in the first place and was a friendly, distant presence throughout. The Regional Advisers, Ann Steele, Melissa Simpson and, above all, Robert Grant read and commented on the developing work. Jan Haenraets, Head of Gardens for the Trust, though just in post when I began the book, was always thoughtful and receptive, and the Gardens Assistant, Veronica Barrington, was warmly supportive and promptly found and sent me all the additional information or research material I requested. I'd also like to note how much I appreciated Terri Baxter's patience and organisational skills in the early days. Tony Lord deserves a bouquet for his sedulous correction of any and every hint of sloppiness in nomenclature.

Special thanks to the Head Gardeners, who were so ready to show me round, answer questions, and review drafts, often going well beyond the call of duty. It is largely on account of the days I spent walking around their gardens that I shall put this book aside with a real feeling of regret. The garden historian Christopher Dingwall also requires a grateful mention for kindly taking time to spend a memorable spring afternoon at the Hermitage, introducing me to its history. My thanks, also, to my publisher and editor Piers Burnett of Aurum Press; to Brian Chapple, who was principal photographer and went wherever I suggested, even to small and less famous gardens, and remained cheery, even when it rained; and to Peter Ward the designer, who worked willingly with me searching for the best way to present this book, his talent has contributed hugely to it.

Acknowledgements are also due to the Trustees of The National Library of Scotland (www.nls.uk) for permission to print the Bauchop plan of Newhailes, and to the Ordnance Survey for sections of old maps showing gardens. The map on page iv is by ML Design. My thanks also to Ken Bushe (www.kenbushe.co.uk) for generously allowing me to include his image of one of his paintings of the Orchard at Barry Mill.

In the course of researching this book, I used many reports and studies of the individual gardens, landscape surveys, and articles, including back issues of the Garden History Society's magazine and *Journal* as well as general books on Scottish gardens. The recently published *Dictionary of National Biography* (Oxford, 2004) in its easily searchable electronic form, supplied many details about the owners and gardeners. For my introduction, I drew heavily on inspiring studies such as Sheila Mackay's *Early Scottish Gardens* (Edinburgh, 2001), Forbes W. Robertson's *Early Scottish Gardeners and their Plants 1650-1750* (Tuckwell Press, East Lothian, 2000), *Thomas Blaikie* by Patricia Taylor (Tuckwell Press, East Lothian, 2001), and the reprint of John Reid's *The Scots Gard'ner* of 1683 (Mainsteam, Edinburgh, 1998) with its wonderful, contextually enlightening introduction by Annette Hope. Information was often conflicting, but it is not the fault of the many authors and experts I consulted, if I have come to injudicious conclusions.

Francesca Greenoak

PICTURE CREDITS

All photographs except those listed below were taken by Brian Chapple

The following photographs come from The National Trust for Scotland Photographic Library:

Pages: 9 (top right), 18, 29, 34, 40, 62-3, 79 (top right), 82, 83 (bottom right), 88 (bottom left), 93 (top right), 98, 103 (both), 106, 110 (top left), 120 (top left), 125 (bottom left), 133, 147, 163 (top right), 170 (three), 171 (top right), 172 (top and bottom left), 179 (both), 182, 183 (top left), 186 (top left), 198, 199, 200 (both), 204, 207, 208 (bottom left), 213 (top centre).

Also from The National Trust for Scotland Photographic Library:

By Paul Adair. Pages: 113, 114 (top left and bottom right).

By John Boak. Pages: 100-101, 112.

By Nicola Ferguson. Page 9 (bottom right).

By Allan Forbes. Pages: 26-7.

By Mark Leman. Pages: 176-177 (bottom),

By David Robertson. Pages: i, ix (top right), 130, 180 (top left), 195.

By A. Smith. Page 180 (bottom left).

By Harvey Wood. Pages: 66, 75 (bottom left), 167.

Other photographs are by:

John Anderson. Pages: 136-7 (three), 138, 139 (bottom right), 142, 214 (top left).

Mike Bolam. Page 169 (bottom left).

Ken Bushe. Page 102.

Duncan Donald. Page 23 (top right).

Robert Grant. Pages: 201, 210-1 (all).

Francesca Greenoak. Pages: vi (top right), vii (top right), 10 (bottom left), 39 (bottom left), 48-9, 53 (top right), 54 (bottom left), 55 (bottom right), 58-9 (both), 60, 61 (both), 81 (bottom left), 107, 117 (top left), 124-5 (top), 128, 129 (bottom right), 139 (right, top and centre), 140, 141, 143, 146 (both), 148, 150, 151, 162 (top left), 163 (bottom right), 166, 174-5 (three), 184-5, 186-7 (middle), 190-1 (middle), 194, 208 (bottom left).

Bryan Hinton. Page 41.

Nick Hoskins. Pages: 28 (top left and bottom left), 30, 31.

Steve Kellett. Pages: ii-iii, 152-3 (both), 154, 155 (top left).

Caileen Maclean and Ian Turnbull. Page 158 (both).

David N. McIntyre. Page 135.

Callum Pirnie. Pages: xiii, 56.

Clare Reaney. Pages: 132 (top left and centre and bottom left), 134, 214 (top right).

Isla Robertson. Pages: vi (top left and centre), vii (top left), viii (top centre), ix (top left and centre), xii, 28 (right), 32-3 (both), 35 (top left and bottom left), 36 (both), 37 (both), 50, 51,52, 53 (bottom right), 54 (top left), 94 (top left), 122, 124 (top left), 126, 127, 129 (top right), 132 (top right), 155 (top right), 156, 157, 168-9, 176 (top left), 178 (top and bottom left), 180 (bottom right), 181.

Russell Shanks. Pages: 118-9, 123,

Melissa Simpson. Page 172 (bottom right).

Anne Steele. Page 205.

George Taylor. Pages: 13 (bottom right), 212.

David Wheeler. Pages: 20, 21, 23 (top left), 24 (top left and bottom left), 25 (top right), 213 (top left and right), 214 (bottom right).

Sinclair Williamson. Page 149 (four).